Because of Amy

How My Daughter's Death Gave Me Life (And How Your Pain Can Free You Too)

Rita Henry

Cover Design by Erika Brask

Words and Music by CRAIG LEE FULLER

© 1975 (Renewed) UNICHAPPELL MUSIC INC. and MCKENZIE MUSIC

All Rights Administered by UNICHAPPELL MUSIC INC.

All Rights Reserved

Used by Permission of ALFRED MUSIC

Publisher's Cataloging-in-Publication (Provided by Cassidy Cataloguing Services, Inc.)

Names: Henry, Rita (Rita Teresa), author.

Title: Because of Amy : how my daughter's death gave me life (and how your pain can free you too) / Rita Henry.

Description: Des Moines, IA : Inner Prosperity, [2025]

Identifiers: LCCN: 2025912207 | ISBN: 9798218603830

Subjects: LCSH: Henry, Rita (Rita Teresa) | Children--Death--Psychological aspects. | Loss (Psychology) | Bereavement--Psychological aspects. | Grief--Psychological aspects. | Mothers and daughters--Biography. | Resilience (Personality trait) | Self-actualization (Psychology) | Spiritual life. | Self-perception. | Self-esteem. | Happiness. | LCGFT: Autobiographies. | BISAC: SELF-HELP / Personal Growth / Happiness. | FAMILY & RELATIONSHIPS / Death, Grief, Bereavement. | BODY, MIND & SPIRIT / Inspiration & Personal Growth.

Classification: LCC: BF575.G7 H46 2025 | DDC: 155.9/37092--dc23

"Relationships are the richest, most rewarding, and often the most challenging aspect of our lives. From heart-wrenching losses to the peaks of Love and joy, relationships offer us deep insights into ourselves, and into the nature of life itself. They show us, often in brutally honest ways, what we most need to heal in ourselves."

~Rita Henry

This book is for you, Dear Reader.

I am you. Just not lately.

The messy roller coaster of life brought me to my knees more ways than I can count. But all the pain, heartbreak, and contrast helped me connect with myself at a level I'd always wanted but didn't know was possible.

The same can be true for you.

You're not the bad decisions you've made or the painful experiences you've lived through. And you're not alone in any of it.

Thank you for witnessing my journey. I can't wait to see where it takes you. We're all stronger together.

Praise for Rita Henry

"This book will change your life if you're willing to allow your heart to open a bit more with each word."

~Sheila Franzen, The Spiritual Geek

"This journey is universally resonant; almost everyone will see pieces of their own life reflected in your story, which is precisely what makes your book so impactful and valuable."

~ Jonathan Parker, PhD

Contents

Part Four

World Peace Is An Inside Job

Part Five

Doing My Work Gave Me My Life

Content Warning

This book contains topics that may be sensitive to some readers, including, but not limited to: emotional abuse, trauma, sexual abuse, and death of a child.

Be gentle with yourself along the way.

For extra support and resources you can use while reading, head to resources.ritahenry.com/because-of-amy.

By the way

I've purposefully capitalized some (but not all) instances/versions of the words "Love" and "Truth." A capital "L" or "T" denotes using these words in their highest vibration of pure consciousness rather than a limited perception based on fantasy or misunderstanding.

Foreword

"Prepare yourself for a journey. This book is more than a story—it's an invitation to heal, to grow, and to discover that you are not alone."

Your life began under the guidance of those who themselves were shaped by lives of struggle, pain, and confusion. These guiding figures, our parents, inherited their beliefs and so-called "wisdom" from generations before them, each passing down their unique mix of triumphs, losses, and disappointments. Add to this inheritance the weight of financial struggles, health crises, emotional traumas, abuse, abandonment, and the occasional dose of misfortune, and it becomes clear why so many find themselves grappling with the complexities of simply being human.

A dear friend of mine often says, "Everyone goes through life with a large sack of rocks over their shoulder." He's speaking of those heavy burdens we all carry: the heartbreak of fractured relationships, the relentless pressure of stress, the scars of emotional and physical abuse, the sting of betrayal, financial instability, and the uncertainty of health. These are the stones that weigh us down. Life, with its twists and turns, often throws these burdens our way when we feel least equipped to bear them.

For over three decades, I've been privileged to walk alongside Rita, witnessing her remarkable journey as a confidante and friend. Over time, our bond has deepened, forged by the stories, struggles, and insights we've shared. In my own fifty years of counseling, having conducted over 50,000 one-on-one sessions with people from all walks of life, I've come to recognize one undeniable Truth: our struggles connect us far more than they divide us.

It's a strange paradox—this universality of pain. We often feel isolated in our suffering, convinced that no one else could possibly understand the depth of our struggles. Yet when we dare to share our stories, we discover echoes of our pain in the voices of others. These are not conversations we typically have at the dinner table. Much of what we endure remains hidden behind polite smiles and closed doors. And so, we carry on, believing we are alone.

That's what makes the book you're holding a rare and invaluable gift. Rita's story is not merely a recounting of personal trials—it's a mirror, reflecting the hidden parts of your own journey. As you walk alongside her, she invites you into her most intimate revelations, creating space for your own memories, perhaps long buried, to resurface.

You may find yourself laughing with her at times, and crying with her at others. Her vulnerability and authenticity will remind you of the humanity we all share, the battles we fight, and the triumphs we sometimes overlook. But beyond the shared moments of recognition, Rita offers something even more profound: the lessons and wisdom she has gleaned from her struggles. These are Truths born not of theory, but of lived experience.

Think of Rita as a gentle guide, walking beside you as you navigate the rocky paths of your own life. Through her words, she will hold your hand through the tough spots, whispering encouragement and insight when you most need it. She will take you deeper than you may have thought possible—not to overwhelm you, but to help you unearth the healing, strength, and wisdom that have been waiting within you all along.

Prepare yourself for a journey. This book is more than a story—it's an invitation to heal, to grow, and to discover that you are not alone. Rita's reflections will inspire and empower you to lay down some of the rocks you've been carrying and to walk a little lighter, with newfound courage and hope.

--Jonathan Parker, Ph.D., 2024

Preface

I've been "doing my work" since 1996 when I checked myself into a hotel room to unpack the death of my nine-day-old daughter, Amy.

What do I mean by "doing my work?" I mean the process of recognizing how I got where I am and releasing the blocks keeping me held in excruciating pain.

Doing your work means leaning into your past—the stories, held and charged emotions, bullshit beliefs, misunderstandings, core issues, and traumas you don't even know are there—to heal and transform them so they no longer knock you on your ass every time your kids ask you for something you can't (or don't want to) give them. It's looking at where your pain is stored (mentally, emotionally, physically, or astrally), bringing it into present time, and clearing it so you can be happy without waiting for everyone in your life to go to therapy first.

When I left that hotel room having sobbed myself raw trying to make sense of Amy's life—and her death—I started a journey into connecting with myself at a level I'd never known before. A journey that led me to shift my consciousness, change my brain, increase my awareness, and heal the pain of my past—from being sexually assaulted at ten years old to the death of Amy and everything in between.

Once I did my work, *everything* in my life changed. (This book is proof.)

Now, because I've faced my own trauma, I help other people release stored pain from *their* past. I make it easier for people like you to do *your* work by holding a safe space for you to show up exactly as you are (messy hair, pissy pants, penchant for choosing people who will only ever break your heart, and all), naming Truth, and making energetic shifts that quiet the noise so you can make peace with your troubled past and create a life you frickin' Love.

This book is for everyone struggling to change their life, stuck in pain, wanting everyone else to change so they don't have to.

It's also a gift to my past self, the part of me struggling to make sense of this insane world. The woman who didn't know having compassion for herself was even an option. Who gave until it hurt and then gave some more, unknowingly losing herself along the way.

She wasn't ready to hear it, by the way. Not for a long time. Maybe you are. Maybe that's exactly why this book made its way to you.

Pain is Inevitable, Suffering is Optional
Introduction

Nine days after my identical twin daughters were born fifteen weeks premature, my daughter Amy died in my arms.

It was 10 p.m. on a Sunday when Amy's doctor tucked us into a private room in the Neonatal Intensive Care Unit (NICU). He removed the tubes and wires keeping her alive so I got to hold her for the first—and last—time.

As I cradled her tiny 1 lb 1.2 oz body, I bawled for the loss I was facing. I wept in gratitude for the depth of Love shared between me and my precious baby girl.

Astonished she was strong enough to live so long without her breathing tube and life-giving support, the doctor kept coming in to check on her. He didn't expect that level of vitality for such a tiny little girl who'd already been through so much.

A little over an hour later, Amy took her last breath.

For months after she died, I'd press into the bruised ribs on my right side as a reminder that she was real. The jolt of pain from where I carried Amy in my womb was one of the only physical reminders that I had after we'd buried her.

Until it too faded.

While I was incredibly grateful for my three other children, my arms felt empty, aching to hold Amy.

Being with Julia, Amy's identical twin sister, was bittersweet. I was infinitely grateful she survived and Loved seeing what Amy would've looked like. And yet, Julia was a constant reminder Amy was gone.

I wanted Amy to grow up with her sister and two older brothers. To be part of our family.

When she died, I was devastated. Crushed. Cut off at the knees. My brain couldn't function carrying the all-consuming heaviness of grief. The only reason I was able to get out of bed in the morning was because I had three other children to take care of.

I wasn't wrong for wanting Amy to live beyond those chaotic nine days.

She wasn't wrong for dying.

Had she survived, her non-functioning kidneys and eventual grade-4 brain bleed would've required round-the-clock care. It would've crushed us financially when we were already drowning in debt.

Still, I wanted Amy alive and in my arms.

I fought reality, rowing my boat upstream in white water rapids without a life vest. It was tumultuous and I wasted tons of energy refusing to accept my daughter's death.

And the longer I fought, the longer I delayed my healing.

Until I accepted the devastating reality that my daughter was dead, I couldn't get to the other side. I couldn't see the absolute gift her life—and her death—had given me: an invitation to show the fuck up and live *my* life.

Unknowingly, Amy's death brought up shit tons of pain that had nothing to do with Amy dying

By the time a psychiatrist diagnosed me with situational depression, it wasn't just Amy's death bubbling to the surface. Though I had no idea I was doing it at the time, I was fighting reality in almost every aspect of my life.

I wanted to believe I was happily married, that I had a happy childhood, that I felt fulfilled at work, and that I Loved myself.

And in many ways, all of that was true.

But I was also tripping all over myself to make everyone else happy before I allowed myself to be, thinking their needs were more important than mine. I was unaware of all the ways I'd been taught I wasn't enough. That men were more important than women. That I wasn't lovable.

I completely lost myself at home, work, and with my children. I gave until it hurt and then gave some more in an unconscious attempt to manipulate them into needing me so they'd never leave. I was terrified of feeling abandoned and rejected.

I had no idea I was abandoning and rejecting myself.

I picked a partner who wasn't on the same page as me. A man who refused to get a job "because I could earn more," but who only took on additional household chores when I broke down sobbing in the laundry room, at an absolute breaking point, crushed by the weight of all it took to raise three kids, run a household, and work a full-time job.

A man who refused to shop at box stores or buy anything other than brand-name cereal—even when we were hundreds of thousands of dollars in debt and I had to cash out my entire 401(k) to pay for the hospital bills and to keep food on the table.

A man who didn't appreciate what I did for our family. And, since his priorities didn't align with mine, he regularly responded with bitterness, anger, and resentment when asked to help out.

That's not to say there weren't happy times. It's not to throw the blame on Nathan. At all.

Because the thing is, I picked him. And it took me more than a couple of decades walking on eggshells and re creating my childhood norms to see it clearly.

I *thought* I wanted an equal, loving partner, someone to love, value, and respect me. But that's not the dynamic I created, and it's not how I taught him to treat me. I'd basically married a re-creation of my dad, a workaholic who didn't trust women, wasn't open-hearted or loving, wasn't kind (even to himself), and who couldn't see or appreciate himself, let alone his partner.

And even when Nathan did show me love or buy me flowers, I couldn't take it in because I didn't think I deserved it.

I didn't know it yet, but the reason I was suffering in all my relationships was because *I was in them*, which makes sense when you look at my childhood.

Pain is inevitable, suffering is optional

While there were happy times, I was raised in pain and insanity.

Pain felt like grabbing the decades-old cozy sweater from my closet. Sure, I had to look past the holes in the elbows, food stains, frayed edges, and the fact that it looked like shit on me. But it was comfortable. It was my normal. I was used to it.

In my childhood home, my dad's anger ran the show while everyone else walked on eggshells, desperate to avoid setting him off.

He'd make up rules and change them on a whim, telling us, "If you don't like it, there's the door," while Mom stood by sobbing, begging him to change his mind. He never did.

While my siblings fought against his rageful, controlling ways, I became the perpetual angel. Even so, it didn't save me from his insanity.

As a teenager going through the greasy hair phase, my dad forbade me from washing my hair more than once or twice a week. He said it was a waste of water and shampoo. I'd rush home after school to wash and dry my hair before my dad got home from work so I wouldn't be humiliated at school.

Think about being told you're not worth the cheapest shampoo on the market or the couple minutes of water it takes to use it. That you're not deserving of basic resources.

That was my dad. A controlling asshole running amok, scarred by being emotionally abused while he was growing up during The Depression.

My entire relationship with him can be summed up in one story.

My dad was pouting around the garden, complaining to me that none of my brothers wanted to go canoeing with him. I knew I could lift a canoe onto the top rack as well as any of my brothers. Eagerly, I said, "I'll go canoeing with you, Dad. Let's go."

"No. You're a girl."

I was devastated. I heard the message loud and clear. My dad didn't love me, my brothers were more important than I was, and I wasn't enough. I wasn't lovable. I wasn't worth choosing.

That tender spot affected me long after my dad refused to go canoeing with me. It followed me into my marriage, my job, and my relationship with my children.

It felt like shit, but when I started leaning in and doing my work, I saw it as a gift. My feelings about my dad's asshole behavior showed me where I needed more self-Love and more self-confidence. They revealed my core issues of abandonment and rejection I didn't even know were there. In time, the tender spots showed me the places I had yet to heal. And they helped me uncover all the ways I was abandoning and rejecting myself.

As I started to see all the ways I didn't have my own back, I stopped giving my power away to everyone else. I began to heal my belief that I was only lovable if someone else loved me. I stopped waiting for other people to love, value, and respect me.

As I leaned in to do my work, I finally saw those feelings of "I'm not enough," and "I'm not lovable" for what they were: the flashy billboard in Times Square begging me to pay attention to what was up for me to heal.

In doing my work and healing from my past, I came to believe I chose my mom and dad as my parents because I didn't think I deserved to be treated any better.

Through my sometimes horrific childhood, I got slammed by my core issues of abandonment and rejection a bazillion times over. Then, as an adult, I re-created my childhood normal, getting my ass kicked again and again until I started doing my work. That's when I finally saw what I was doing and why. It's when I learned to lean in and face those core issues head on.

And only then could I make a new choice.

It's the same for you. As a child, you were innocent. You didn't deserve the shit that got thrown your way.

But now that you're an adult, if you're unhappy with your life or your relationships, if you can't be open-hearted and accepting no matter what's thrown your way, or you think "those assholes shouldn't be that way," the good news is, you're the only one who needs to change.

When you're ready to live an empowered, joy-filled life—even if you don't know how—unpacking and healing your past will free you from the triggers kicking your ass today.

Part One

You Learn Everything Through Contrast

As near as I can tell, we're on this planet to evolve. And we do that through contrast.

Contrast is the experience of opposites. You only know dark because you've seen the light or cold because you've accidentally touched a hot stove.

You can't appreciate your Lover's habit of throwing their socks in the middle of the living room as soon as they get home until they die and you never get to nag them again.

And you might not see the Truth of what you're doing—and why —until you've so thoroughly lost yourself trying to make sure no one else will abandon and reject you that you're in too much pain to keep ignoring all the ways you're abandoning and rejecting yourself.

Contrast helps us appreciate what we have. It teaches us where we need to lean in so we can evolve. It's our greatest teacher and it's essential for our growth.

But often, it feels like shit.

That's ok. The pain the contrast brings up is just showing you what's up for you to heal. On the other side of digging into that pain

Because of Amy

is the life you've always dreamed of creating for yourself. You just have to be courageous enough to face the traumas, triggers, held emotions, misunderstandings, and stories you don't even know you're telling yourself first.

Chapter 1
Avoiding, Pretending, and Denying Aren't the Same as Freedom

My mom suffered a nervous breakdown before I was born. She couldn't function. As part of her recovery, her doctor told her she needed something positive to focus on and that she should have another baby

That baby was me.

I was born seven years after my closest sibling. I was supposed to save my family, to make them happy, and fix the shit no one wanted to talk about. And I sucked at it.

I couldn't stop the phone being ripped off the wall or the police being called. I couldn't force my dad not to kick my brother out of the car to hitchhike the six hundred miles home. I couldn't even get my parents to console me after I was sexually assaulted at ten years old, and because I knew that, I didn't even try.

When my birth didn't make everything better, mom and dad went to counselor after counselor and they all gave the same advice. They all told my dad he should have never had children.

Considering I was the last of five, I was always glad they did have kids. And yet, my parents' unresolved pain radiated through every facet of our lives.

The normal you know

The earliest memories I have of my dad are from when I was four years old when we lived in Chicago.

At one point when he didn't have a job, he'd take me to the library and drop me off in the kid's section to pick out books. Some time later, he'd come back to get me and we'd go home to split a can of chicken noodle soup.

Other times, down in his workshop, I'd strap on my roller skates, racing back and forth across the concrete floor, looping around the support beam and back, completely left alone to entertain myself while Dad completed his latest project.

And once, I remember him packing his tiny, bluish-gray, hard-edged suitcase, telling me he was leaving and I'd never see him again.

I was terrified. Crying, I drew him picture after picture of trees, flowers, birds, clouds, and the sun, tucking them into the suitcase to take with him so he'd remember me.

I begged him to stay, but he walked out without so much as an "I love you."

It felt like my world was coming to an end. Mom was my only means of safety, support, and stability, and she was losing her shit on the daily. For two weeks, she was on the phone with my grandma and Aunt Ruth, sobbing.

Then, one day out of the blue, Dad was home and we were all supposed to pretend like nothing happened. So we did. We never spoke about it again (no matter how many times he left).

Even at such a young age, even though it was confusing, I knew not to ask any questions. Navigating Dad's depression, wild mood swings, and explosive rage was sheer hell for everyone in our family.

We learned to avoid anything that might make him angry. The problem was that Dad was angry—a lot. It didn't matter what you did or didn't do, he'd find reasons to rant. He'd make shit up.

He'd rage because my brother's hair was too long or because my sister came home minutes after curfew. He'd scream at my brother for taking too many showers. He'd keep track of everything he thought you'd ever done wrong on some mental laundry list he'd throw back at you any time his nervous system was out of whack.

At times, I'd hide in my armoire to escape the explosive fights between him and my siblings.

And, more often than not, Mom failed at being the peacekeeper we wanted her to be. As Dad raged, she was either silent or in tears. Once he left the room, Mom ranted about how, even though he went to church every week and said the rosary daily, he wasn't being a good Catholic. He was being an ass.

On the rare occasion she attempted to stand up to him, he raged even more.

Most of the time, she lived in denial, pretending shit wasn't hitting the fan. Or she'd shut down, focusing on getting through the latest turmoil—as if getting through the current fiasco was all it would take to make things better. It wasn't.

After the dust settled, we'd all go back to walking on eggshells, waiting for the next bomb to drop. It always did.

And, even though we all knew it was shitty, wrong, and painful, it was our normal. It was a secret we were all in on, an unspoken rule to never talk about Dad's rabid outbursts outside our home (or in it). Even my childhood best friend had no idea my dad was emotionally unstable and mentally ill—or the hell I faced growing up.

But I didn't know anything beyond the insanity. My parents were authority figures who had full power over my life and everything I did or didn't do. I trusted them.

In my mind, I had no reason not to.

As a child, you're at the mercy of the adults in your life

When you're a kid, the adults in your life are basically God. Your safety literally depends on their ability to meet your needs. If you're lucky, they feed you, water you, put a roof over your head, and wipe your tears when you cry.

But, if you're anything like me, the adults in your life were far from enlightened.

My dad was a mean son-of-a-bitch. And apparently, he only abused those he really loved. Around his co-workers, neighbors, and fellow churchgoers, he was charismatic and charming. But, inside the family, he had four moods: controlling, cruel, depressed, or just existing—except on the rare occasion when he was in nature and happy.

At home, if the wind blew in the wrong direction, he'd give us the silent treatment for days on end. I'd manipulate him into talking to me again by striking up a conversation whenever a neighbor stopped by. It always worked.

Even then, instead of getting pissed at him, I was just relieved he was finally talking to me again. Because as shitty as he was, our whole house gave our power away to Dad, trying to convince him to love us. We knew he was a wounded fuck. We knew he got off on power plays and controlling us. But it was our normal.

Instead of standing up to my dad, my mom used my brothers as her counselors, telling them all the terrible things he did or said. When my brothers stood up to Dad on Mom's behalf, she'd throw them under the bus and side with my dad to "keep the peace."

She did the best she could with what she had, but my mom didn't know how to stop the abuse and dysfunction. She couldn't see the impact her choices had on us kids.

By not having her own back, her actions taught me over and over again how little I mattered. They taught me how to take care of others at all costs, but that I wasn't worthy of the same care and thoughtfulness. I was disposable.

Once, when I was ten years old, my twenty-year-old brother Charles chased me through a neighbor's yard into an alleyway, threw me onto the concrete, sexually assaulted me, and threatened to kill me if I told anyone.

I was fucking pissed. Instead of going to my friend's house as planned (and as he thought I would), I doubled back around the block to avoid my brother, snuck in the front door, and told my parents anyway. When I did, my dad immediately shut down and my mom started sobbing hysterically. They couldn't comfort me. Thankfully, they took me to their friend, Father Daniel, at the monastery who told me it wasn't ok and it wasn't my fault. And, for a short time after, my mom made sure if Charles was going to be around, I was never alone with him.

Growing up, Charles took the brunt of my dad's rage, and despite pretending to laugh it off, it messed him up. After high school, he joined the Air Force, fell deeper into drugs, and then injured his knee and was honorably discharged.

After that, he never had a job. His "friends" only stuck around when he had money. And his drug use continued to get worse and worse. His life was going nowhere fast.

My dad was in over his head. In his controlling, asshole way, he tried to "set boundaries" by throwing Charles out of the house and forcing us to cut all ties.

The owner of a hell-hole apartment down the alley behind us let Charles move in for a while. It tore my mother up to watch her son in this self-destructive spiral. She did her best to feed him in a desperate attempt to make everything better.

But one day, my mom couldn't take food to Charles because my dad was home and would wonder where she went. I was her only option.

She sent me with a plastic grocery bag of food, alone, down the back alley to feed the brother who had sexually assaulted me.

I felt like a sacrificial lamb being sent into the lion's den.

I remember walking down the alley, opening his kitchen screen door, tossing the bag of food on the floor, and sprinting back home, my heart pounding and body shaking. Charles was strung out on the floor in his living room, totally incapable of chasing after me, but that didn't stop the terror and pain that came from my mother putting me in harm's way.

She'd throw me (or my siblings) under the bus at the drop of a hat if it kept my dad from getting angry. Still, Mom was my source of Love. She supplied the only safety, nurturing, protection, and support I experienced, and I Loved her fiercely. I would do anything to protect her—the only lifeline I had for making life tolerable—and I mean anything. Even standing up to my father.

When I was eleven, I came home to find my mom standing in the living room sobbing and holding the back of her head.

"What happened?"

Mom sobbed, "Dad pushed me."

My 6'4" dad had shoved my petite, 5'2" mom and she'd fallen into the corner of the TV stand, gashing open the back of her head.

Filled with rage, I met my dad toe-to-toe. I screamed. I cussed. And I let him have it. Even though I barely came to his chest, he stood there in the middle of the room, head hung, unsure of what to do with himself.

"You will NEVER touch her again. This is not fucking ok." I swore at him and didn't care. He needed to know he would never lay an abusive hand on my mom again.

And while he never did, the mental and emotional abuse continued.

Avoiding, pretending, and denying aren't the same as freedom

My dad had more than a few health issues. He went to the hospital a couple of times for pinched nerves and bleeding ulcers, but he never got help for his mental health (not that anyone cared about mental health back then). Whenever he'd fall into a deep depression, he'd just blame us.

While we were in Chicago, Dad quit working for three years, forcing Mom to get a job as a teacher's aide at a local high school to pay the bills. He refused to drive her to the job even though he was the only one with a driver's license and, with everything stirring in the late '60s and early '70s, there were at least six cops on campus every day. Mom walked the six-plus extra-long blocks to get there, alone.

He also refused to take her to the grocery store, so after work or on weekends, she'd walk a few blocks with her folding shopping cart, buy food to feed five of us for the week, and drag the groceries home —sun, rain, cutting wind, or mountains of snow.

The two main pillars of our family were insanity and instability. Even during short periods of calm, you knew it wasn't going to last.

It was a lot to live with, so by the end of high school, I didn't know what to do, but I knew I couldn't stay with them in Dubuque, Iowa.

I never considered a career that would suit me or fit my personality. I was so thoroughly disconnected from myself that I had no idea what I even wanted to do. My dad told me I should go into computers since that's where the money was. So I did.

Going on college visits would've required time and effort from my dad to drive me there, and that wasn't going to happen. But a nice young woman from the American Institute of Business (A.I.B.) visited our high school and told me about their double major in Computer Science and Accounting.

It was a two-year program that essentially went year-round. Since a four-year college seemed out of my league financially, and I didn't know if I was smart enough to attend one anyway, I settled on A.I.B. without ever having seen the campus.

Year-round school meant I'd never need to move back in with my parents. I didn't need any more convincing than that.

So, two weeks after I graduated high school, I started college for the summer quarter.

The day before I was supposed to leave, my dad told me he wasn't going to take me to school after all. He simply "didn't want to."

I had no idea how I was supposed to get to college the next day. Mom still didn't drive, so that was out. I cried and cried, begging Dad to take me, but it was futile.

After completely losing my shit, I started making phone calls trying to figure out how I could get to Des Moines on Saturday to start classes on Monday. Finally, I came up with a plan. I'd take a taxi to the bus station, hop on a Greyhound bus into the city, and from there I could take a cab to my dorm.

It sucked. I wouldn't be able to bring my kitchen stuff, bedding, or even all the clothes I'd need. But at least I'd be able to start college on time with the essentials on hand.

As soon as Dad found out I had a plan that didn't include him, he agreed to take me, swooping in like a knight in shining armor come to save the day.

What an asshole. Still, relieved that I didn't have to worry about transporting myself to and from the bus station, I let him drive me the three hours and forty-five minutes to campus. The whole way there, we pretended like nothing ever happened, just like we always did. When we arrived, we picked up my apartment keys, unloaded my stuff, and said our goodbyes. Dad was finally gone. I never had to live with him again.

But I was far from free.

Because avoiding, pretending, and denying your feelings may feel like freedom from those feelings. But it's like clinging to a lifesaver during a never-ending hurricane of your own creation. Even if you make it to the eye of the storm every once in a while, you're still going to get pummeled over and over and over again until you acknowledge and unravel the storm itself.

More than my mom's chin

Everything I did with my dad, from the library to hanging out in his workshop was never about me. It was always about what he wanted. Still, I tied myself in knots, desperate for his attention, silently begging him to love me.

I'd spend hours by his side pretending to give a shit about things like his stamp collection, asking questions I didn't care about and listening to him drone on about this one or that one. At one point I even started my own collection trying to win his affection. It was short-lived.

Through it all, I learned that men were more important than women, that women were responsible for men's happiness, that men would always get a hall pass and never be held accountable for their actions or inaction. I learned I wasn't worthy, that I didn't matter, that I had to abandon and reject myself in order to survive and that I couldn't have my own wants and needs. I learned to survive on crumbs of attention.

And I didn't even know it.

I'd inherited my mom's chin and my dad's Love of nature. But I also got my mom's tendency to walk on eggshells trying to keep the man from getting angry. My family's belief that men are more important than women. My dad's workaholic tendencies.

And I played that shit out over and over and over again.

Just like the drawings I slipped into my dad's suitcase before he left us, I packed all that shit up and brought it with me into my adult life—unknowingly re-creating the painful experiences I knew in all my intimate relationships.

Those misunderstandings, unprocessed trauma, and freeze responses kept me locked in my childhood, re-creating my past long after I thought I'd left it behind.

Chapter 2
It's No One Else's Job to Love You

I was a virgin when I married Nathan.

Both of us were raised Catholic. We were taught sex before marriage was a sin. But, both his grandma and my mom's step-sister had had a child out of wedlock. So, the shame, guilt, denial, condemnation, and terror of anything sexual were woven into the fabric of our households growing up. It's all we knew.

My mom would go so far as to change the channel when things got racy on "The Love Boat." Mind you, this was the late '70s, so "racy" meant the Doctor discussing with his love interest whether or not he'd wear socks to bed (with no mention whatsoever about what they'd *do* in bed).

Nathan's mom once reamed us out for hanging out in a bedroom with his siblings. We were laughing and joking, having a good time and she came in fuming about how we "should be in the living room." As if hanging out in a bedroom was sinful.

Before getting married, I knew next to nothing about what sex was supposed to be like. Yet, after walking down the aisle at twenty years old, I was suddenly supposed to be good at it? Awkward.

Nathan and I never talked about sex. We just did it. No foreplay. A little kissing, and as soon as he entered me, we were done and it was time to clean up. Then, he'd roll over and go to sleep, leaving me craving more intimacy.

Sex was never about my pleasure. I didn't even have my first orgasm until I was around thirty. But I never saw it as settling because I didn't know any better. I was grateful for the crumbs of attention. I loved the closeness sex created and I loved being with Nathan, fully giving myself to him, and feeling our shared connection.

I thought I'd found a man who would "complete" me, someone who'd "make" me feel loved, valued, respected, and seen. And all the while, I believed it was my job to please Nathan, be the good girl I was raised to be, and lose myself trying to make him happy. I was so steeped in being a good Catholic girl, I didn't see the double standards, judgments, or shame. I didn't know I was ashamed of my body or blindly denying my sexuality.

I'd tell anyone who asked that I was happily married.

But I basically married a slightly better version of my father

When I first met Nathan, he lived across the hall from my friend Deb's new apartment. He came right over and introduced himself and started hanging out with us pretty regularly. He'd just graduated college, didn't have "real" friends he wanted to hang with, was super lonely, and hated his job. But he seemed like a good guy, and after a while, I encouraged Deb to go out with him.

I didn't know he had his eye on me. Looking back, it's obvious now.

Nathan wanted to spend time with me whenever he could. He offered to take me to mass on Sundays as an excuse to be alone with me. When we officially started dating, he took me dancing, wooing me with his ability to twirl, dip, and spin. He'd happily go shopping with me—even garage-saling now and then. He joined me on adventures to visit my mom and dad in Dubuque or my brother in Chicago.

Because of Amy

He put care, focus, and effort into trying to "get me." He chased me with gifts, using his artistic abilities to create and mail packages to my parent's house when I went home for a holiday. One Valentine's Day he sent me a giant basket with a stuffed animal lobster under plastic (like in the meat department), a fish cookbook, starfish, fish netting, and a huge homemade card.

When his mom met me, she encouraged him to get me a promise ring. "Scoop that one up," she told him. So he did.

After we were married, everything changed.

At a wedding or event where there was dancing, he would do one or two dances with me at most. And he'd always do it with an "I'll appease you, but I don't want to make you too happy" attitude.

When he did go to the store with me, he'd chastise me for looking at all my options and feeling into what I wanted. He wanted me to be like the "hunter" he was: go in, get the thing you want, and get out.

Eventually, he stopped going with me when I visited my family. He hated going, and my dad hated him. (I was actually grateful, because balancing trying to please my parents and him at the same time was a nightmare.)

Nathan constantly told me, in a bazillion different ways, that I was wrong. Wrong for being cold when he wasn't. Wrong for choosing healthier foods. Wrong for how the spices I cooked with smelled. Wrong for wanting to create sacred spaces in our home to snuggle into. Wrong for wanting more intimacy in conversations and in the bedroom. Wrong for wanting to do things as a couple or as a family.

I had absolutely no idea that I'd re-created my childhood normal. I'd married a re-creation of my dad: a workaholic who didn't trust anyone, who wasn't open-hearted or loving, who wasn't kind (to me or himself), and who couldn't see or appreciate his partner.

But Nathan and I could've been in a crowded room blindfolded and we still would've picked each other.

It didn't matter that he "flipped a switch" when we got married. We were both playing out our childhood patterns in a way that made us a perfectly nauseating match. Our marriage was exactly what I was taught love should be, and his behavior was what I thought I deserved. I was willing to put up with his anger, bitterness, and resentment because being treated poorly was my comfort zone.

It's how I treated myself.

I gave my power away, just like I'd been taught

From the time I met him, I encouraged Nathan to do what he was passionate about—to pursue his art and find joy in creating, even when he wasn't financially supporting our family.

I didn't know what I was passionate about, but I wanted him to pursue his dreams. I thought it would make him happy. And I wanted him to be happy because I thought that would make me happy.

But he was too shut down to be happy. He couldn't be grateful. He couldn't see beyond his own suffering and disappointment.

And, as painful as it was, I ate that shit up. His bitterness, anger, and resentment felt like coming home. It fed my abandonment and rejection, unconsciously reminding me of sitting idly by pretending to care about stamps to "win" my dad's affection.

And just like the stamps, I had to connect with Nathan on his terms since he wasn't interested in any of the things I cared about. I took whatever crumbs I could get—even though it meant losing myself along the way.

We went for walks because he "had to stretch his legs anyway." We went out to eat once in a while because he "had to eat anyway." And I could model for him because, as an artist, he "wanted to draw anyway."

I might as well have been a wooden stick figure model, both for the lack of connection the experience provided and for the way he drew me with a Barbie-thin waist and cartoonishly huge breasts in place of my A-cups.

He called it "artist's liberty," but it never felt like liberty to me.

He'd tell me he married the homecoming queen. He'd ogle over my legs and ass. Yet, as an artist, he drew me in a way that clearly stated his preferences—and they were not how I looked. In fact, they weren't how the majority of women on this planet look either. It was a fantasy no one could live up to.

But I put my blinders on and jumped through hoops, losing myself and ignoring all the ways he didn't respect women (not that he was taught to). His mixed messages fed my insecurities and supported every conclusion I'd come to as a child; I couldn't accept my body because I wasn't enough.

Unknowingly, I'd become my mother, busy pretending things were different than they were.

Years after we were married, Nathan took a nude modeling class at the art center. His instructor was desperately looking for models, so Nathan asked if I would step in.

I agreed. The female body is gorgeous, and I wanted to use the experience to release and heal the feelings of inadequacy, shame, and judgments that I had about myself and my body.

At every class, before I took my clothes off, I'd introduce myself to the students. I'd tell them, "I share a love of art, and while I struggle drawing stick figures, I love being a part of the creative process."

I told them that, through modeling, I was learning to accept myself more deeply.

Modeling empowered me to face my fears and accept myself exactly as I am—stretch marks from having four babies and all. Self-acceptance helped me to face and move through challenges in my life more quickly.

As a model, I used each pose as a meditation to share Love with everyone in the room. I showed up vulnerably and open-heartedly, cheering them on. People loved it.

Word got out that I was an incredible model, and colleges in the area started calling me, paying top dollar to get me on the schedule. I always made it a requirement to have Nathan join the classes, using it as time to connect with him.

Years later, after leading a group meditation, a woman introduced herself and shared that she had drawn me at the art center. She gushed that it was the best picture she had ever drawn. In fact, it was framed and hanging in her parents' home, and they loved it too.

What started off as an unhealthy desperation to "win" my husband's attention eventually became a super healthy way for me to heal. It helped me face the shame I carried around my body taught to me by my mom, the Catholic Church, and society.

It was an "Accept your body and your life exactly as it is or you'll stay stuck in those shitty judgments" kind of practice.

Still, none of this happened overnight.

It took ages to learn that it was my job to Love, value, and respect myself whether Nathan loved, valued, and respected me—or not.

I flipped back and forth. Sometimes I could see the Truth, bringing Love and compassion to myself for all the times I didn't know any better. Sometimes I would fall back asleep, feeling shame for my squishy mom-tummy, exploding at my kids, or giving my power away to Nathan.

I was getting my ass kicked by life

I desperately wanted to pretend I was happily married, but that meant I had to overlook all the ways I was being disrespected. I had to ignore all the ways I wasn't chosen or made a priority and keep my blinders on to all the ways I fought for crumbs.

I was the major breadwinner in our family. And, after the girls were born, between Julia's continued healthcare needs and taking leave for six months, to say money got tight was an understatement. We were swimming in debt. Every month was a struggle.

Nathan refused to ask his parents for help. Instead, I cashed out my entire 401(k), penalty and all, and asked my mom for help. Thankfully, she loaned us money here and there, but it didn't stop the sky-high interest rates from eating us alive.

Meanwhile, during that time Nathan completely stopped working and I eventually started running my own business. He'd tell me to take on more clients, "because I could earn more." And he'd only get a job when we needed to prove steady income so we could buy a new (used) van—and stayed with it just long enough to get the loan.

At the same time, he set "strong boundaries" around his "working hours," carving out a 9-5 schedule to work on his art and only helping with family stuff after that.

That meant, on top of everything else, we had to pay for child-care, which, for our three children, cost more than our monthly house payment. But I wanted to support his dream of being an artist, so I readily agreed.

Only when I broke down sobbing in the laundry room about how I couldn't possibly take on more clients *and* do laundry *and* get groceries *and* mow the lawn, would he begrudgingly agree to take over one of the tasks.

Then, when he was the one grocery shopping, he'd refuse to go to box stores or buy anything but name-brand cereals. He'd also crank the AC in the summertime and tell me I was wrong for being cold or to "just put on a sweater."

I felt like the only one trying to get our family out from under the crushing debt as I bought used clothing for myself and the children or skipped my own dental checkups because we couldn't afford them.

On top of all that, my periods used to knock me on my ass, which would frustrate Nathan to no end. When I wasn't 100 percent game on, he'd shut down. I'd ask him to sit with me when I was feverish and throwing up, and he'd get gruff. Obviously annoyed, he'd bring me water or a snack but refuse to hang out with me. It was like he wanted to punish me for not feeling well.

His time and attention were conditional, dependent on me

upholding impossible standards and energy levels. There was no room for me to be human or real. It was painful.

But he was innocent. And so was I.

We were both just playing out what we learned as children—and we didn't even know it. Again and again, I'd try to please Nathan in hopes that it would finally leave me feeling safe, happy, and satisfied. But since it required me to lose myself, it didn't and never could.

And, boy, did the Universe make that clear (though it took me a while to see it).

It's no one else's job to Love you

I wanted Nathan to be my answer. I wanted him to make me happy, fulfill my needs, and be able to read my mind about what those needs even were (because I sure as hell didn't know).

But he couldn't.

Even if he'd told me he loved me every minute of every day, showered me with gifts, spent endless amounts of quality time with me, or drew me exactly how I looked, I wouldn't have been able to take in his love because *I didn't believe I deserved it.*

If I didn't have to chase after him to feel lovable or if he didn't bring out my triggers of abandonment and rejection, I wouldn't have chosen him in the first place. That's what I thought love was.

He wouldn't have chosen me if I didn't jump through hoops trying to earn his affection, because that's what he thought love was.

And without even knowing what the hell we were doing, we re-created our childhood norms by triggering the shit out of each other over and over and over again. Me, scrambling for connection, and him using work (that he wasn't getting paid for and was too ashamed to share with the world) as a "socially acceptable" way to distance himself from me.

Wanting someone else to love, value, and respect you will never work if you don't already Love, value, and respect yourself. It's not sustainable.

It's not wrong to want someone else to love you.

But it's no one else's job to Love you. It can't be.

And until you know that for yourself, you'll keep chasing unavailable partners, blaming them for your unhappiness, denying all the Love that *is* shared with you, and lying to yourself about how good—or bad—your relationship really is.

Luckily, this wasn't the end of the story

But it did get worse before it got better.

Chapter 3
This is a World of Insanity

I 've always loved children. I started babysitting my neighbor's newborn when I was ten years old. Being with kids was fun. Being a caregiver was easy. But babysitting didn't prepare me for the magnitude of becoming a parent.

Babysitting never taught me how to get my newborn baby to latch on for breastfeeding or about the searing pain from my nipples becoming the delivery system for milk. Or how hearing a phone ring in the grocery store could make my milk come in as if I'd just heard my baby cry, massively leaking through the little round pads in my bra while standing in the checkout line.

Babysitting didn't keep me from losing myself to my children's wants and needs.

But, honestly, even before I had kids, I'd already lost myself trying to please Nathan, work, and my parents. I was raised to keep the peace, to do backbends whenever someone else needed something—regardless of how I felt about it.

None of that changed when I became a mother. I didn't lose myself any more than I already had. I just had more shit to do.

Back then, it was standard to return to work four weeks after giving birth, and I did. But, with my two boys, it took at least six months for us to adjust and find a routine. And even with a routine, life was hectic.

From the time my alarm went off at 5:45 until my head hit the pillow, I was running on fumes, doing my best to embrace the chaos.

That meant trying to make sure everyone, including Nathan, had everything they could possibly want to be happy—while ignoring my own wants and needs. Skipping breakfast in favor of feeding the boys and packing their lunches for the day? I thought that's what made me a good mom.

By the end of the day, I was exhausted, emotionally drained from a full day at work, and completely tanked if I let my blood sugars get too low.

While I was breastfeeding there weren't accommodations to pump at work, so I'd make a mad dash home to relieve my full and aching breasts. I'd be gutted when I went to pick up Matthew and, as soon as he saw me, his meal ticket, he'd transform from a happy, smiling baby to a screaming, angry monster demanding to be fed.

And when there were two of them, I'd end up wrestling with a toddler while carrying my newborn and the heavy-ass diaper bag into the car and then the house. (God forbid I ever had to make two trips.)

On top of that, we found out the hard way that the peace and sanity of our household depended on getting the boys exercise every day. So, unless Nathan made mac 'n cheese with frozen peas, I had to make dinner and then do whatever I could to exhaust the boys before bed.

I'd play tag around the island wall separating our kitchen from the living room or chase them up and down the small hill in our back-yard while Nathan cleaned and reset the kitchen.

While I appreciated Nathan feeding and watering the boys when he could or would, he wasn't emotionally nurturing. He begrudgingly came upstairs to serve meals, but rarely ate with us. He was judg-mental when I decorated for birthdays and the holidays. And he couldn't find joy during trips to the zoo or hanging out in the back-yard because he felt obligated to "do the family thing."

No matter how hard I tried, I couldn't make him happy (at least not sustainably).

But getting lost in everyone else's needs—especially when I didn't know my own—was as easy as finishing the whole bag of potato chips (even though you only wanted one). To break the habit, I'd have to do more than just pretend next time would be different.

I twisted myself into a pretzel trying to "earn" Nathan's love and attention, desperate for him to be my answer, convinced I needed his approval to feel safe, chosen, and lovable. I ignored my wants and needs as if they didn't exist because that's what I thought made me a good mother, wife, daughter, and employee. I stayed busy decorating the house with smiling snowmen, red hearts, or cute pumpkins, blind to how conditioned I was to give until it hurt and then give some more.

I denied myself, pushing every frustration down deeper and deeper until I exploded just because someone did something as silly as leaving the cap off the toothpaste. And even then, I'd just apologize for my existence and go right back to playing house.

For the longest time, I genuinely believed things were good—or at least comfortable. So I didn't stop to question what I was doing or why. I didn't see the warning signs or pay attention to all the ways I was living out my childhood as an adult. After all, there were moments of open-hearted Love. There were times I remembered my hunger for Truth and curiosity for the world and why I was in it.

But ultimately, I was too busy trying to get by to notice much of anything.

What I thought mattered...didn't

In February of 1994, I went on my first Caribbean cruise with Nathan, a friend from work, and her husband.

At the time, I worked in the IT department of an insurance company—solving problems, developing new systems, and keeping the old systems up and running. I managed frustrated users who demanded overnight reports or panicked when systems crashed.

The stress was never-ending.

Management set impossible deadlines and redlined when we couldn't meet them. The workload made it impossible to take a deep breath or to feel relieved—even when we did finish a project. My nervous system was constantly in hyperdrive, and I often felt like crawling out of my own skin.

It was as if I was in my childhood yet again, jumping through hoops, doing anything I could to please my dad. Another circumstance to be sure, but the pattern was exactly the same.

And, still, I didn't see it—until I did.

On that cruise, Nathan and I signed up for a Discovery Scuba Dive. After a short training on shore, we were handed little baggies of dry dog food to feed the fish.

Swimming out to the coral reef felt like being dropped into a Disney movie. Giant stingrays glided past. Hundreds of fish in all different shapes and sizes swirled around in a dazzling riot of color and motion.

Everyone else threw handfuls of pellets for the fish to swarm. I took a single pellet between my thumb and forefinger and held it out. One bold fish nibbled away as I ran a finger along his side.

I couldn't contain my joy. As he chowed down, the bubbly underwater sounds, bright colors, and salty water enveloped me in a watery cocoon.

A deep inner knowing washed through me. "This world doesn't give a shit about my world."

The fish don't care about overnight reports. The stingrays don't know about dishes or laundry or having dinner on the table by six o'clock. The currents don't try to control their flow.

Later on, I clung to this experience and the wisdom it offered: *There's more to my world than I'm aware of. My pain isn't the only story. I don't have to be consumed by it.*

I'd been taught to walk on eggshells, to give my power away, to feel like what I did was never enough. I'd been so steeped in pain, I didn't even know I was stuck in it.

I left the ocean floor forever changed.

What a relief to know there was more to the world than what I experienced day-to-day. To figure out I was still writing my story—it wasn't over yet. To know my feelings didn't have to control me. To feel light, even in the darkest dark. To know, even when I'm consumed by fear, there's still Love.

I didn't know how much I'd need these lessons in the coming years. I didn't know they'd help me do my work to heal the pain from my past and anchor into unconditional Love for myself. I didn't know everything I was hungry for would come from connecting with myself.

Rather than paying attention to my feelings and dealing with them, I kicked the can down the road for a future version of me to deal with. The Universe would continue to have its way with me until I finally couldn't ignore it anymore.

Then the girls were born and my whole world imploded

When Nathan and I got married, I wanted five children.

We both grew up in households with five kids, so it made sense to us to do the same. Then the reality of working full time, momming full time, and keeping our house up and running full time hit—and we decided three would be enough.

I found out I was pregnant six months before we'd planned on having our last baby. That wasn't a huge deal. But when the ultrasound tech said, "There *they* are," my heart stopped.

They? As in, more than one?!

Immediately, I went into a freeze response. My mind was absolutely blown. We were already so overwhelmed with the boys that the thought of adding not one but *two* more kids at the same time felt impossible.

Because of Amy

For weeks Nathan and I kept asking ourselves, "How's this gonna work??" over and over again. Only after settling a bit, could I finally sink into the excitement of adding twins into the mix of our household. I don't know if Nathan ever did.

In the second trimester, we bought and refinished wooden bunk beds from a neighbor, moving the boys into a shared room and making space for the twins.

But I didn't have time to nest after that.

At twenty-four weeks, I knew something was horribly wrong when, out of the blue, I was struggling to catch my breath and my legs were going numb when I sat down.

I called my doctor every day for a week. I told him my symptoms and begged him for another ultrasound, which was a basic standard of care for twins, even then. His reckless advice was to, "Take up to four Tylenol a day," assuring me it "wouldn't hurt the babies." It didn't help.

The day after I hit twenty-five weeks (minimum viability for a pregnancy at the time), at 5:30 in the morning my contractions started—and to my horror, didn't stop. Nathan had just gone for a run and I was going into labor fifteen weeks early.

I called the doctor again. This time, he told me to meet him at the hospital.

Then I called our neighbor who graciously came over to take care of the boys while I threw some things into an overnight bag and waited for Nathan to get home. I was supposed to have three more months before I needed to pack a go bag.

The streets were mostly empty as we drove to the hospital in silence, both of us too scared to talk. By 7:00 a.m. I was tucked into a room where they gave me a drug to stop the contractions. The only thing it did was make me feel horrible.

The contractions kept coming.

On average, babies are born with around a quart of amniotic fluid in the sac surrounding the little nugget(s). When my girls were born, I had over five *gallons* of amniotic fluid in the sac with them.

I didn't know it, but I had a condition called polyhydramnios, which means I had too much amniotic fluid surrounding my babies. Only one percent of pregnancies present as polyhydramnios, and mine was extreme.

My body had decided it was time for everyone to get out of the pool.

Three hours after I first called him, my doctor finally showed up. The only thing he said when he got there was, "RITA, THE WATER!" with a look of sheer terror on his face.

Ten minutes later, at 8:47 and 8:48 a.m., the girls were born.

The image of their tiny little bodies is still burned into my memory

Julia came first, the heavyweight, at 1 lb. 8.5 oz., while Amy weighed a mere 1 lb. 1.2 oz. Considering the size of my fluid-filled abdomen, it was shocking to see how tiny the girls looked in the hands of the doctors.

Miraculously, they were born right after the morning shift change so both Julia and Amy had their own neonatal doctor. They were each placed on an Ohio bed and immediately intubated to help them breathe. The doctors and nurses worked to stabilize the girls and clean them up while I finished delivering the placenta.

As they whisked the girls out of our room and to the neonatal intensive care unit (NICU), Nathan and I held each other, sobbing, terrified for our precious girls.

The nurses then helped clean me up, put me in a wheelchair, and took me to the NICU to see them. But as soon as I stood up to take the four steps to Amy's side, I blacked out, my body in shock from having just given birth. Thank goodness a nurse was there to catch me just before I hit the granite floor.

When I came to, it was a relief to see the girls alive and utterly heartbreaking to see them in such a fragile condition. They were placed under a lamp, eyes covered, their delicate skin smothered in gel to keep the heat in. We weren't even allowed to hold them.

Later that afternoon, Dr. Bhavsar told us that the girls had a forty percent chance of survival. I decided right then and there to believe—to *live*—as if both girls were going to survive. I couldn't imagine the alternative. It was too devastating.

Over the next few days, as the girls fought for their lives, we fought to stay afloat in the chaos.

We were peppered with paperwork from the hospital, insurance, government, and more, scrambling to take care of our boys at home. And desperately trying to come to terms with what had happened and what we needed to do next.

Despite the major toll giving birth had taken on my body, I did my best to take care of my family. I split my time between the boys and our newborns—who each had their own beds and weren't always near each other. I spent as much time as possible by each of their sides, always feeling like I was falling short on being enough for anyone.

In the middle of it all, the NICU staff gave us a crash course in premature babies. After a while, Nathan refused to read any more on the subject, saying it depressed him too much. In contrast, I needed to know everything. The doctors and nurses joked about adding me to their staff.

For a few days, things were stable as we adjusted to this new normal. Then concern for Amy grew. And with each day that passed, the concern became more intense.

On the Wednesday afternoon after the girls were born, one of the doctors called me and a NICU nurse, Cheryl, into a consultation room. I was at the hospital alone.

Dr. Sahu sat me down and told me Amy's kidneys never "turned on" due to her premature birth and now toxins were contaminating her body.

"You can't live without functioning kidneys," he said.

He gently went on to explain that Amy had also suffered a grade-

4 brain bleed the day before, which meant, "If she does survive, she'll need constant care since her brain isn't fully functioning."

My heart dropped into my stomach and I completely shut down my feelings. I didn't want to believe it. As he explained Amy's medical status, I asked him analytical, logical questions in return. It was my attempt not to succumb to despair, to not completely shatter from the horror. And a part of me wanted to save him from my pain.

How did you discover the brain bleed? Can it heal?
Where is the brain bleed and how will it impact Amy's future?
Is there anything we can medically do so she'll live?
What will her quality of life be if she survives?

Dr. Sahu patiently listened to and answered my questions. He connected with my spirit, never once failing to truly see me, even through the pain of being the bearer of this awful news. His gentle presence was the exact support I didn't know I desperately needed.

When finally I ran out of medical questions, I fell silent. There was nothing more to say, nothing more to do. I finally understood what he was saying. My daughter Amy was going to die.

Before Dr. Sahu left, he stood up and offered me a hug. I fell into his arms. Because of him, I wasn't utterly alone in my pain. He was my lifeline. I didn't have to walk through hell alone.

With tears in her eyes, Cheryl told me, "I've worked with Dr. Sahu for over twenty years, and I can count on one hand the number of times he's ever given anyone a hug."

It meant the world to me.

The way that Dr. Sahu met me and the pain I carried gave me the courage I needed to share the news with Nathan.

I had to give Amy permission to die

I drove home in a daze, unable to digest the news that my daughter was going to die.

Because of Amy

My biggest nightmare was now my reality. I was devastated. Absolutely crushed. My entire body felt shut down and frozen.

I don't remember telling Nathan the news. I don't remember eating dinner or tucking my boys into bed. I don't remember driving back up to the hospital while Nathan stayed at home with them. But late that night, I do remember being alone by Amy's side. I had to be with my precious baby girl.

Things quieted down in the NICU at night.

There were still twenty-eight other babies and the night staff surrounding me, but Amy's Ohio bed was tucked into a corner of the open room and the lights were dimmed. So I had a little privacy as I alternated between sobbing, being on the verge of sobbing, and talking aloud to Amy.

Her nervous system wasn't fully developed and she was super sensitive to touch, but I gently placed my hands on her body and faced the profound sorrow of what it would mean to live life without her.

My voice shaking, I told her how much I Loved her.

The rawness of this unimaginable loss swept through every cell of my body in a rush of emotion, swallowing me whole. My heart broke all the way open in a way it never had before.

This little girl was already such an intimate part of me, it felt like trying to learn to live without oxygen. It was like I'd been handed one of the most precious gifts I'd ever received and I was being forced to give it back before I'd had the chance to fully know her.

Standing before her Ohio bed, connecting with her beautiful Soul, it hit me. I had to give Amy permission to die.

She didn't need my permission. And I didn't want her to die. But I knew in every cell of my being that I needed to face Amy's death. I couldn't pretend it wasn't happening. I didn't want to impose my will onto this beautiful newborn child. I didn't want to be the one holding her back, tethering her to life, or keeping her from doing what her Soul needed to do.

Giving her permission was my way of saying, out loud, "I'm surrendering the need to control whether you live or die." Because, inherently, I knew I couldn't control what was going to happen anyway. I had to accept what was happening—no matter how much I hated it.

Over the next few days, her health continued to decline and, after eight days of horrible unknowns, it became obvious to everyone that Amy wasn't going to make it.

She died nine days after she was born, at 11 p.m. on a Sunday.

The NICU was quiet. We were given a private room and, for the very first time, I got to hold Amy without the tangled lines of life-giving support. I was simply a mother holding her baby and sharing my infinite Love.

The doctor kept coming in and checking on us. He was astonished that she went on living and breathing on her own for so long before she died. He didn't expect that level of vitality and life force for such a wee little one who'd already been through so much.

For over an hour, I held Amy, sobbing.

I sobbed at the loss I was facing. I cried tears of gratitude for the Love I shared with my precious daughter. And my heart broke open as both the pain and gratitude crashed through me.

This is a world of insanity

This is a world where people make reality wrong. Where they get stuck thinking their daughter shouldn't have died, even though she did. Where they build walls around their heart to keep them safe and never let anyone in, even though they're lonely. Where people throw anger at those they love most because it's the only place they can safely express themselves—and they don't have the tools to do it any other way.

It's a world of insanity.

And insanity means acting from a place of disconnect. It means you're not connected with yourself, with your Soul, and with what you want and need—because you're too locked in your pain, old patterns, misunderstandings, and ego to even see you're doing it.

Waiting for the world or other people to change so *then* you can be happy will only cause you to suffer.

You can't make sense of insanity. The only thing you can do is the work required to end your own.

You do that by naming Truth, seeing the patterns, bullshit lies, and misunderstandings you're playing out, and releasing the charged emotions that you don't even know are there, so you can finally stop letting them run the show.

You do that by accepting your life—exactly as it is, even when you don't like it.

You do that by getting honest about what you're doing—and why —so you're no longer a ticking time bomb waiting to explode because you don't know you're running from your past.

It took me more than a decade to get there, but after I leaned in and did my work, I didn't have to keep getting thrown around by the pain, trauma, and triggers. I could see them in Truth and know they were just showing me what was coming up for me to heal.

And life is so much sweeter on the other side.

The first step is accepting the world as it is, insanity and all, and deciding who you want to be in response. Believe it or not, it's a choice.

For me, that meant accepting Amy's death—even when I didn't want to.

My daughter's death is the hardest thing I've ever experienced

I didn't know it at the time, but grief truly is a process. And I hadn't even begun to touch the deepest core of it.

For a couple of years, the mental and emotional toll of losing Amy haunted me every day. I was devastated. I'd given her permission to die, but I wasn't ready to face the reality of what that meant. I wanted Amy to grow up with Julia. I wanted her to be part of our family and get to know her brothers. So many of my dreams died when she did.

Simultaneously—and guiltily—after her grade-4 brain bleed, a part of me was relieved that Amy died. As the breadwinner of our household, I was overwhelmed thinking about how we would've cared for Amy and still functioned as a family. I couldn't wrap my brain around the mental, emotional, physical, and financial resources we'd need (and didn't have) to give Amy the round-the-clock care she'd require.

Even without Amy I still had my other children to provide and care for. My boys deserved to have a Loving mother at home, but for four months Julia was fighting for her life in the hospital. I couldn't be in two places at once. I had no idea how any of it would play out or how it could possibly be ok.

Watching her identical twin sister, Julia, grow up was a blessing—and yet painful. I had a front-row seat to what Amy would look like had she survived.

Every time Julia cried (and eventually laughed), I knew what Amy would have sounded like. Every time Julia wore that look of focused determination whenever she tried to prove herself to her brothers, I knew Amy would've done the same. And every time I celebrated Julia for birthdays or milestones, I was reminded that Amy was gone.

As much as Julia filled me with joy, the constant reminder was devastating.

And there was no one I could talk to about any of it. They didn't get it.

When I eventually went back to work, if I brought up Amy's name it was like I'd just taken a shit in the middle of the room. People innocently didn't know how to respond. They wanted to pretend it never happened.

Because of Amy

But it did. *Amy happened.* Her life and death were such a huge part of my life. Even though she only lived for nine days, she changed me forever.

Part Two

You Think You're Further Along Than You Are

Ninety-five percent of what you do is subconscious and unconscious.

The filters, lies, misunderstandings, BS beliefs, held emotions, traumas, and triggers you don't even know are there will kick your ass over and over until you meet them toe-to-toe so they can be cleared.

Why? Because, until you face the pain, you'll never be free—and the Universe has your back. It'll amp up the pain a bazillion times over so you can finally heal the core.

Chapter 4
You Deserve More Love, Not Less

After Amy died, Nurse Cheryl led us into a private room to bathe and dress her for the first and last time. As tears flowed, Cheryl got in Nathan's face, surprising us both as she said, "Over fifty percent of couples who lose babies get divorced. Keep talking to Rita."

She was right.

Nathan compartmentalized Amy's death. At her funeral, he carried her tiny white casket up the aisle alone, looking like his daughter just died. But it wasn't until four years later when someone pressed him about his experience, that he openly sobbed for the first time. For the most part, he was stuck in a freeze response, unable to process his feelings.

I, on the other hand, openly grieved, which frustrated Nathan to no end.

In the months that followed, I would ask him a million times why he wasn't feeling the same way I was, why Amy's death wasn't crushing him like it was me.

He'd tell me, "I just didn't know her like you did."

While I never understood his lack of emotions, I knew our family benefited from him being exactly where and as he was. By not processing the loss, he was able to keep our family hobbling along. Grocery store runs, caring for the children, cleaning up the kitchen, running errands, paying bills, and even shoveling snow when we got pummeled with mountains of the white stuff... It was a lot.

Without his robotic ability to get shit done, moving through life like nothing ever happened, we wouldn't have survived as a family.

A day after Amy died, while Nathan and I were visiting Julia in the NICU, a social worker came to talk to us. She took us to a nurse's station and proceeded to go over the necessary steps we had to take now that Amy was gone.

There was follow-up paperwork galore, including notifying the Social Security office that the previous request for Social Security numbers for the girls now needed to be updated to include Amy's death. Then, there was the death certificate itself, along with a blur of hospital protocols and bills for Amy's care.

Paperwork overwhelmed me at the best of times. Thank goodness Nathan was there to guide me through it all because, drained and emotionally raw, I didn't have it to give.

But I did hear the social worker loud and clear when she talked about possible next steps. "One option is to freeze Amy until we know the outcome for Julia."

Her words gutted me. I knew she was doing her job and giving us options. And yes, we were already a hardship-case and financially drowning. Bearing the expense of two funerals with money we didn't have would've added jagged rocks to the bottom of the cliff we'd already fallen off.

It didn't matter.

"NO," I roared before Nathan could even respond.

I hadn't yet discovered energy work, but it was very much an energetic thing.

Freezing Amy felt like telling the Universe I believed Julia might die too. I had zero tolerance for that thought. Just as I had for Amy before learning her death was inevitable.

I couldn't live as though Julia was going to die.

Planning Amy's funeral sucked

I wanted to create an honoring tribute to Amy, but there were so many decisions that needed to be made.

What time should everything happen? Which prayer cards with what images should we hand out? What casket do we get? What do we feed everyone who's painstakingly traveled here from out of town?

It was such a fucking whirlwind. And I already had nothing to give. My mind was blown by all the details. Like how the smallest casket they had was two-and-a-half feet long. It dwarfed Amy, who was only twelve inches tall when she was born.

As we grieved, we coordinated with our church a short viewing for Amy before mass, a potluck put together by the Rosary Society after mass, and the readings and songs that would happen in between.

Nathan wrote a short and sweet obituary. We lined up the hearse, picked the time for the wake the night before at the funeral home, and found and chose a space in the baby section of the cemetery. We begged them to hold the grave site next to Amy's for a couple of months, just in case. Because, while I refused to freeze Amy, I wanted the girls to be next to each other if the unthinkable did happen.

And, since these were the days way before social media and texting, we still had to tell everyone who needed to know that not only were the girls born early, but that Amy had died.

I called my mom and sister-in-law, asking them to pass along the information. Nathan called his parents, and they let the siblings and cousins know. I told a friend at work who told all my co-workers.

After making all the decisions about when everything should happen, what to feed everyone, and how the visitation and day of the funeral would play out, all that was left was to live it.

It's a miracle I even knew what to wear, let alone that I remember any of it. I was in such a deep freeze response, the days are hazy to me now. Bits and pieces stand out like an instant recall, but for the most part, I just remember the all-consuming pain.

Because of Amy

At the wake, it was surreal standing in line to visit with people after they'd walked by Amy's tiny little casket. Many of them froze when they saw me, tripping over what to say. Others came to me, falling into my arms, sobbing, unable to hold themselves together.

I found it so odd and yet completely natural to console them.

Their grief, triggered by my daughter's death, left them with no capacity to see my pain. It was all about them. But I was used to losing myself and giving until it hurt, then giving some more. I spent more than I had during the wake and funeral, comforting others and ignoring my own pain.

The entire two days I felt empty and hollow; on the verge of sobbing or silently weeping.

We had an open casket an hour before mass for people who couldn't come to the wake the night before. The service started with Nathan carrying Amy's closed white coffin up the long aisle and setting it on a table near the altar. After mass, we loaded her into the hearse and a trail of cars followed us to the cemetery a couple of miles away.

Someone had given the girls matching soft, white bunnies when they were born. Amy was buried with hers inside her casket.

Once the tiny box was lowered into the ground, everyone took turns throwing flowers onto it.

The beautiful blooms covering Amy's casket were a stark contrast to the pain I felt. While I love flowers and was grateful for the outpouring of Love people shared with these gorgeous bouquets, my daughter was dead, and no posy was going to make that any better.

I found some comfort being surrounded by people who Loved and cared about me. But most people had no idea what I was going through. How could they possibly understand?

At a viewing, photos often fill the room, highlighting the person's life, showing who they were, what they experienced, who they loved. I didn't get photos of Amy's first day of school, her first birthday party, her college graduation, or her wedding. I didn't get to know my daughter. I didn't get to see what she was like.

And I was drowning in it.

Other times, people were a distraction. They wanted to know details and asked endless questions to support their own processing and satisfy their curiosity. Being gracious with them took precious energy I didn't have.

Over and over, I told people when the girls were born, why Amy died, how Julia was doing, and on and on. I didn't know how to tell them that sharing was sucking the life force out of me.

Even the simple question of, "What can we do to help?" was overwhelming. I was so tapped out I had no idea what I needed or where to start.

What could anyone else do?

My family of origin was especially limited in their capacity to help. Mom did the best she could, but the most emotional support she ever offered me as a child was to get a wet washcloth and wipe away my tears. That wasn't going to cut it in the face of my daughter's death.

Still, she came to the funeral and stayed with me for a handful of days after, until Dad got pissed because she wasn't at home to make his meals.

My dad was stuck in his own childhood and never acknowledged I had a daughter who died. He didn't come to the funeral and never said a word about it after.

Dr. Sahu, who first told me that Amy was going to die and supported me through it, shocked the nurses by attending Amy's funeral. I hugged him once more and cried as I thanked him for coming. It meant the world to me to have him there to honor Amy's life and death.

And through it all, Julia was still fighting for her life in the NICU.

It tore me up to take time away from her to tend to the bazillion details of planning a funeral. All I wanted was to be by her side. And yet, I wanted to honor Amy's life and death.

I felt responsible for picking out a casket, keeping everyone up to date, and tending to their emotional needs—while also making sure my boys were cared for. The expectations and grief crushed me. I felt alone in it all.

Opening to Love is really hard… until it's not

Going through the motions, I forced myself out of bed in the mornings, took care of my boys the best I could, and always made time to visit Julia.

All the while, I carried the guilt of being relieved Amy had died. Her death created breathing room for me to focus on my other children. And her death was a cavernous pit of despair I constantly fell into.

Shutting down and closing my heart wasn't an option. My other children needed me.

At the same time, I was drowning in a sea of paperwork and financial ruin, feeling alone in the grief, and completely overwhelmed by taking care of my boys, seeing Julia, planning a funeral, and forcing myself to eat so I could still breastfeed.

I wondered what would've happened if Amy had been my first and only child. Feeling the crushing loss of my daughter's death without the day-to-day pleasure of my other children there to remind me that joy is always an option? It sounded horrible.

My arms weren't empty because I had a five-year-old, a two-and-a-half-year-old, and a newborn fighting for her life, but they certainly felt empty not being able to hold Amy too.

Consumed with shock and totally overwhelmed, at times it was impossible to function. I dropped a million balls I used to juggle. Laundry. Cooking. Regular showers. Anything that wasn't absolutely necessary to my survival went out the window.

Without support, I would've died.

For two-and-a-half months, people from work graciously brought us dinner, lined up babysitters so we could go back up to the hospital each evening, and oh so much more.

But it was uncomfortable accepting that level of support from others. I was *way* more comfortable giving than receiving. I sucked at receiving. Receiving is vulnerable since you can't control what other people give you.

So, while I was infinitely grateful for all the support, it also triggered the shit out of me. I was consumed with the feeling of being unworthy of their generosity. I worried about how I was going to "pay them back." (Eventually, I realized I never could and didn't need to, but it took a while.)

Letting in that depth of Love and support was incredibly difficult. It went against all my beliefs that I didn't deserve love in the first place.

When you're used to living your life a certain way, when you're stuck believing the conclusions you came to when you were growing up, changing can be the hardest thing in the world.

You deserve more Love, not less

You've been conditioned to believe love comes from other people or the things you buy.

Society, companies, and the patriarchy all benefit from your belief that you'll find love on the other side of a new relationship (preferably one that comes with an expensive wedding and lots of dates in between) or with free shipping from Amazon.

You're sold an idealized version of romance from Hollywood, commercials, and the novels you read. But, when you don't Love yourself first, the Love you get from anyone or anything outside yourself will never be enough.

You'll either spend your life chasing unavailable partners, buying shit that doesn't really make you happy, or trying desperately to convince everyone and their goldfish that you're lovable. It's what you're used to. It's what you think you deserve.

But you deserve to be Loved twenty-four hours a day, seven days a week, 365 days a year.

Because of Amy

At the same time, I don't know anyone on this planet who's gotten that. And when you don't receive the Love you deserve, you'll do things like *lose yourself* or *give until it hurts and then give some more*, even though it feels like death by a million paper cuts.

The Truth is, Love is who you are. No matter what you've experienced, gone through, faced, or done, nothing makes you unlovable. There's nothing you have to do to earn Love. You just have to remember that for yourself. That's why you do your work.

Doing your work—releasing held emotions, clearing the bullshit lies, and undoing the misunderstandings you grew up believing—is how you experience more Love.

Chapter 5
You Can Use Relationships to Heal and Grow or Lose Yourself

Before I gave birth to the girls, I didn't realize how unsafe I felt most of the time.

Vying for Nathan's fleeting approval, walking on eggshells to navigate my dad's asshole ways, or living in constant fear of being reamed out by the big-wig client at work who set impossible deadlines and freaked out when they weren't met all sent me reeling.

But after the girls were born, the pressure was a bazillion times worse.

Not only were my boys relying on me to be fed and watered, needing snuggles, baths, and bedtime stories, but for the first six months, I constantly worried about Julia, lost in her every need. I felt helpless.

At any time, something as simple as the common cold could send Julia spiraling. Her underdeveloped lungs and fragile immune system were compromised and her older brothers were walking Petri dishes, bringing home germs from daycare on the daily. Julia still needed to build her reserves. She still had to develop and strengthen her body.

I did everything I could to support her, but no matter what I did, I couldn't guarantee she'd live.

The rawness of having just buried Amy was a literal weight in my chest. It amplified the terror of losing Julia. My hyper vigilance left me on edge, living from one threat to the next.

People would look at me and say, "I don't know how you're doing it all."

But really, what else could I have done? I couldn't just sit around eating bonbons.

While Julia fought for her life, my top priorities were spending as much time as I could holding her, sharing my Love, and feeding her my breast milk so she got the best nourishment possible.

The whole time, I felt completely helpless.

Under "normal" circumstances, my stomach shut down whenever big emotions hit, making it impossible for me to eat. So, while I knew breast milk was critical in the early months because it had the antibodies Julia needed to fight off viruses and bacteria, I had to force myself to eat in order to keep producing nourishing milk.

I heard that if I wasn't eating enough fruits, veggies, and proteins to produce milk, my body would take what it needed from itself. It was a relief. I didn't care that producing this magical milk supply came directly from the nutrients I needed to survive, so long as Julia got what she needed. As long as my daughter was taken care of, the cost to my own body didn't matter.

Giving until it hurt and then giving some more was what I'd always done. At least this time it felt purposeful, like it was something I could do to help my daughter.

And I continued to lose myself—again and again

Being with Julia in the NICU for over four months while she struggled to survive meant I had a front-row seat to just how hard life in the NICU is. Not only were the hospital staff struggling to cover shifts, but while Julia was there, the number of babies in the NICU doubled—an increase they'd never handled before. Day in and day out, any number of babies needed care for serious medical issues.

These precious nuggets might be stable one day and coding

(needing to be brought back to life) the next. As parents and family members, we helplessly rode the rollercoaster of emotions along the way.

Because my heart needed it, I spent as much time with Julia as I could. Nathan hated going to the hospital, so I'd go there alone during the day. He'd join me in the evenings, but often I'd end up staying late into the night.

I found it impossible to leave her side.

During that time, I got to know the nurses, doctors, and other families who spent time with their own critically ill babies. One afternoon, when a little boy coded, the NICU staff kicked all visitors out of the room as they worked to revive him. Everyone except me. They asked me if I would stay and support this first-time, single mom facing her child's death alone.

They knew since I'd been through it before, I could support her.

I didn't even consider my own frail and overtaxed nervous system. Never mind that I was still processing Amy's death or that I was still terrified by the uncertainty of Julia's future. I had to help.

Her son ended up dying. I stood by her side for hours, witnessing her pain, answering her questions, holding her in my heart, and creating a safe place for her to sob.

I remember tenderly leaning in as we stood side by side while she held her son's body and solemnly telling her, "He's here to break your heart wide open."

I encouraged her to bathe and dress her son. I invited her to let the hospital staff take pictures of him so she'd have a precious memento of him later.

I saw myself in her. I knew she felt helpless carrying this burden alone. So I recklessly gave away my presence and Love. I drained reserves I didn't have. It took a huge mental, emotional, and physical toll on me.

Supporting her came at the cost of not only myself but also my ability to take care of my family, which of course pissed Nathan off.

And facing his anger drained me even more. Afterward, I was in bed and barely able to function for days.

Months later, she reached out and told me how much that support meant to her. And looking back, I'm grateful I could be there for her. I don't regret it, but it was fucking hard.

Trying to maintain a stable household was nearly impossible

Nathan and I included the boys in what was going on as much as we could. We'd bring them to the hospital every week or so, and at home, it was all they talked about.

The Sunday afternoon before Amy died, my five-year-old son Matthew told me on the way to the hospital that Amy was going to be a "people bird" in heaven. I was stunned. It was so matter-of-fact. He knew his sister was going to be an angel.

Later on, after she died, my two-and-a-half-year-old son Thomas took inventory of everyone in our family. Mom, in the kitchen; Dad, in the bedroom; Aunt Kay, in the bathroom; Matthew, at the table; Thomas, at the table; Julia, in the hospital; Amy, in heaven with God.

When I showed him a picture of Julia and asked him who it was, he said, "Julia," and then he started crying and telling me that he wanted Julia to come home, "I miss her."

Julia consumed so much time and energy.

She was the anchor we were all tethered to, not as a burden so much as our constant focus. We all just wanted her to get better. We were so focused on her that most everything else fell to the wayside.

Balancing the pressure of Julia being in the NICU while still caring for my sons was intense. Considering the circumstances, we did the best we could, but so much of it was me shoving down the heartbreak and fear while feeling guilty about not doing enough. I barely got to see the boys. I barely slept. I barely held myself together enough to make sure all of Julia's needs were met, to celebrate her wins.

And, thankfully, there were lots of wins to celebrate.

When Julia was born on August 5, she weighed 1 lb. 8.5 oz. and was twelve inches long. She ate five CCs (approximately ⅓ tablespoon) of breastmilk every two hours. Nathan and I were allowed to "kangaroo" with Julia as long as she was doing well (hospital lingo for cuddling with your baby by placing her on your bare chest).

She hit the two-pound mark by September 13, ingesting a tablespoon of breastmilk every two hours via a tube going directly from her abdomen into her stomach.

By October 4, she no longer needed to be on the respirator with the breathing tube. She graduated to using a nasal cannula with blow-by oxygen, and we could see her beautiful face so much better after that.

She passed the three-pound mark on October 14, attended the NICU Halloween party as an Easter bunny wearing her pink Cabbage Patch doll pajamas, weighing in at four pounds, and began breathing all on her own by November 14.

Nathan and I took her home on Thanksgiving Day (November 24, 1994), and by December 8 she weighed a whopping six pounds. In comparison, Matthew and Thomas both weighed over eight pounds when they were born.

And while I was incredibly grateful to have Julia home where I could enjoy her smiles and spunk without having to spread myself so thin between home and the hospital, it was also scary.

We had to figure out how to keep her safe without the support of the hospital staff. We had to hook her up to monitors every night to make sure she was still breathing. And we had to get into a routine of feeding and snuggling her every two hours to keep her gaining weight and feeling safe.

It took almost two years before we reached some semblance of normal. And even then, "normal" looked completely different from what it had before.

You can use relationships to heal and grow or to lose yourself

And, boy, did I lose myself. Over and over. In too many ways to count.

I didn't just lose myself with Nathan. I lost myself in most every relationship I had.

I lost myself at work, with my family of origin, with my marriage, with my children, and everything in between.

I was constantly making sure everyone had everything they needed to feel settled, without ever considering myself.

Need me to work fifty-plus hours a week and twist myself into a pretzel trying to finish all the reports that won't be looked at for another week, but that you *had* to have today? I was your girl. I'd not only get those reports in on time, but I'd do it with minimal bathroom breaks—because what's the need to pee, really?

Want to come over for a visit? You better believe I straightened the house, cleaning up toys, making sure all the shoes were in the closet and the kitchen counters were empty so it looked like no one lived there (all while raising two boys under five).

Planning a trip back home? Oh, sure, I'll pack up everything needed for the boys and myself (including car activities and snacks) all while pretending away Nathan's pissy attitude about having to come. Once there, I'd walk on eggshells and placate Dad when he vied for my attention and got jealous that I'd need to focus on changing someone's diaper or taking them potty.

I thought I was happy. And in many ways, I was.

But I was so busy "people pleasing" in order to avoid being abandoned and rejected, I unknowingly abandoned and rejected myself.

I didn't know I was living a nightmare. To me, it looked like a dream.

Then again, fantasies and nightmares are opposite sides of the same coin. Neither one is real and both are painful ways to live—because living a lie isn't sustainable.

Losing yourself in the name of pleasing everyone around you will only end in burnout, bitterness, anger, and resentment.

Pretending you don't have wants and needs doesn't mean you don't have wants and needs. Not naming them doesn't mean you'll magically be in a satisfying relationship.

Acting like you have to "give until it hurts and then give some more" to earn your partner's love sucks. Believing you need to jump through hoops to make everyone in your life rely on you so they won't abandon and reject you, isn't the same as Love and freedom.

Every relationship gives you opportunities to heal and grow *or* to lose yourself.

And if you don't have a solid relationship with yourself first, you won't get to the healing and growing because you'll be too busy losing yourself all over the place.

When you're connected to yourself, you're connected to everything

In the weeks after Amy died, waves of deep loss and sorrow washed over me again and again. One moment I'd be present, then I'd remember Amy was gone and fall into a dense fog of grief I couldn't escape.

One cloudy day, I was in the backseat of my friend's car as we were driving down a highway. I was feeling the desolate loss of Amy. Silent tears streamed down my cheeks as the scenery flew by.

Then, as if on cue, the clouds broke open and streams of sunlight came pouring through right when the song "Amie" by Pure Prairie League came on the radio.

"But now you're off with someone else and I'm alone. You see I thought that I might keep you for my own.

Amie what you want to do?

I think I could stay with you
For a while, maybe longer if I do"

I knew it was her.

This song came out in 1972 but somehow made a *huge* comeback right after Amy died in August of 1994. It was like she was talking to me, sitting in the grief alongside me, reminding me I wasn't alone.

As sad as I was that her body was no longer here, I began to notice how she was always with me. Our bond ran deep. It went beyond the nine chaotic days she lived.

I found peace, joy, and solace exploring this strange new connection with Amy.

I began to ask her questions and then pause before hearing her voiceless voice, or an inner "knowing" respond. More often than not, I was surprised by her words.

Amy was feisty and spunky but always Loving and kind. She wouldn't tolerate me arguing for my limitations or being stuck in pain or playing the victim. She wouldn't tell me what I wanted to hear, but always handed me what I needed to hear. Her words were soothing, comforting, guided, and sometimes mouthy.

She'd let me sit in the pain if I needed to, but her voice was a Loving bucket of cold water dumped on my head to wake me up from the grief, sadness, pain, and limitations.

When I was present and connected to myself, I was able to "see" Amy in everything. She spoke to me, reminding me she was always there.

There was no loss.

The spring following her death, I wanted to stop by Amy's grave to bring her a flower before we went to the zoo for Mother's Day. My yellow tulips weren't blooming yet, but when I went into the yard, a single red tulip was waiting for me.

That red tulip showed up for a couple of years after, moving to different places around my yard even though I'd never planted any. It was like I wanted to bring her a flower but she brought one to me instead.

Amy's presence brought me comfort. She showed me what was real, even beyond death. She helped me connect to Love, even beyond the pain, though at first, this new expanded reality was confusing to navigate.

I hated that her body was gone, but when I let go of what I thought life *should* look like and opened myself to what was, the connection I felt to her was—and still is—infinite.

Chapter 6
You're Being Shown
What's Up for You to Heal

F inding a new connection with Amy didn't take away the pain. From the moment I first heard the news that Amy was going to die, I went into a deep freeze response, shutting down my feelings just to make it through the days.

How do you go on when your daughter dies and the world keeps spinning?

As the youngest of five, I watched my siblings experiment with drugs and alcohol while trying to make their pain go away. Deep down, I knew that losing myself in that way was never going to give me what I wanted.

Even at my lowest after Amy had died, getting drunk felt like a fool's game.

One night, when I was getting ready to go to a friend's house, the weight of responsibility and unprocessed grief was paralyzing. For a moment I considered getting smashed. Seconds later, I started laughing hysterically.

I knew all three of my kids would be up at 6:00 a.m. begging to be fed and watered. Being hungover with a raging headache and screaming kids to take care of would only make things worse.

I desperately wanted an escape, but stepping out of reality for an evening wasn't my answer. I just wanted the pain to stop. But, I had no idea that the pain was what I was used to, it almost felt comfortable to me, like an addiction I didn't know I had.

Making a new choice meant not only finding a new way but also breaking out of my comfort zone. It meant acknowledging all the ways my past was influencing my present and processing the trauma so it no longer ran my life.

Stuck in survival mode

During the first two and a half months of Julia's life, people from work generously brought us supper every night. Nathan stepped up and did the usual fill-in grocery store runs for other meals. But, once Julia was home and the meals from my co-workers stopped, I was inspired to give grocery shopping a go. I took my nearly three-year-old son, Thomas, with me.

It was an out-of-body experience. There I was in the grocery store, watching myself but completely unable to make any decisions.

In the first aisle, I saw eggs. *We need eggs*, I thought.

But the huge selection of eggs immediately overwhelmed me. Small, medium, large. A dozen, eighteen. Organic. Free range. White or brown. There were a zillion options.

Paralyzed, I pulled Thomas from the cart and set him on the ground. "We need eggs, Thomas. Which ones should we buy?"

He toddled over to the eggs and carefully grabbed a dozen. I picked them up and put Thomas and the eggs in the cart, feeling accomplished.

In a daze, I finished my shopping, doing the best I could to get the basics for some meals, but the entire time I felt off.

Shouldn't the world have stopped turning since Amy died? And here I was grocery shopping. It was oddly normal, essential to provide for our family, and yet, completely unfamiliar. Something inside me had changed forever. *Who was I after Amy?* I had no idea.

When I got home from the store and unpacked everything I'd bought, I realized we already had eggs in the fridge.

I already knew I needed to lean on Nathan and it was never more obvious than when I tried to get groceries for us.

For two years after Amy died, I was stuck in a perpetual freeze response, living in survival mode, trying to function while Julia was on the razor's edge. I'd go through the motions, but I wasn't really doing much more than running myself ragged and staying busy to numb the pain I didn't know how to process at the time.

I was so used to taking care of others mentally, emotionally, and physically and not having my own back. I'd go, go, go until I couldn't anymore, crashing and burning every six to nine months, so depleted I was stuck in bed for a precious day (or three) with zero energy, terrified I'd never have the strength to get up again. This went on for ages, until I started doing my work.

I didn't know taking up space, unplugging, having a voice, and having compassion for myself was even an option.

You're being shown what's up for you to heal

After Julia came home, I felt fine as long as I avoided thinking about Amy's death, the absence of her growing up in our home, or what it all meant to me.

There was so much going on anyway. It was all I could do not to spend my time worrying about Julia and our finances. I was spread thin loving on and caring for my kids, chasing false deadlines at work as if they were possible, and trying desperately to hold myself together for everyone else's sake.

When Julia was finally stable, I began to thaw. I started to see and feel what had been bubbling beneath the surface all along.

Trauma is anything you've experienced that you couldn't process at the time it happened. So your body locks in the pain until you can meet it, process it, and let it go.

When Amy died, I fell into survival mode. I couldn't handle the massive loss and grief welling up inside. There were too many other things to do, kids to take care of, workplace drama to lose myself in, and pain to dodge so I could live to see another day.

I found out the hard way that avoiding, pretending, and denying your pain doesn't make it go away. It just makes it impossible to be fully present and happy.

The trauma I hadn't dealt with—from Amy, but also from my childhood—unknowingly took up immense space, time, and energy, weighing me down. Until I met it, I was never going to be free. I was going to keep hitting triggers, misunderstandings, and pain until I finally started paying attention and processing the feelings and emotions stuck in my body.

The Universe is generous like that. It'll give you endless opportunities to face your shit so you can finally be free.

When you suppress, repress, and depress your feelings—when you pretend like they don't exist or that you shouldn't feel the way you do—you're either going to explode and project your pain onto others or internalize it and abuse yourself.

But, when you accept those messy emotions and realize they're simply showing you what's coming up for you to heal, they no longer control you.

That's what doing your work is all about.

The feelings, emotions, and even the pain you experience aren't the Truth of who you are. They don't define you. They're just showing you the core issues and layers of trauma you may not even know you have.

And when you get to a point where the pain isn't all-consuming and you're no longer stuck in survival mode, you can choose to process your feelings so they no longer drive your bus, ruin all your closest relationships, and leave you working sixty-plus hours a week to "earn" your worth.

Or, instead of facing it, you can kick the can down the road to deal with another day.

No matter what's going on in your life, whether you've been

sexually abused, raised by a raging asshole, or just lost your nine-day-old daughter, accepting it (exactly as it is) is better than fighting it or claiming it "shouldn't" have happened—even when you hate whatever "it" is.

It doesn't mean you don't get fucking pissed. It doesn't mean you aren't left gutted, heartbroken, disappointed, and in the throes of despair. It just means you accept the raw reality that "it" happened.

Because fighting reality doesn't change reality. It doesn't bring your daughter back or erase the heartbreak. It just keeps you stuck in pain and suffering.

Fighting reality rather than facing it means the pain will show up again and again in different forms, reminding you what's waiting to be healed.

Fighting reality keeps you stuck in the grieving process unable to move forward with your life. You'll end up blaming all your sadness on your divorce from twenty years ago or getting pissed at your boss instead of processing your anger at your dad for walking out the door when you were three years old.

When your daughter dies, there is no solution.

Desperation, loss, hurt, pain, grief, rage, and fear will come up. But if you pretend those feelings aren't there or try to will away the depression and anxiety, they'll eat at you forever (until you finally face the pain). And, despite what they say, no amount of time will heal that.

Whenever you fight the reality of what is, you end up disconnected, unhappy, and miserable.

If you're not open to seeing Truth, you'll get stuck. If you're not seeing reality, you won't be able to move past the grief. You won't know whether you're doing something because you want to or because it's the old pattern of pain you're used to.

That doesn't mean leaning in and seeing Truth is easy. Or that it happens on a predictable timetable. On the contrary, the journey into Truth and freedom from your pain is some of the hardest work you'll ever do.

It requires a death of who you think you are, surrendering the lies you don't even know you believe, and accepting yourself exactly where and as you are—which gives you a totally new experience of Love.

It means allowing yourself to have feelings—even when they make other people uncomfortable.

But once you do your work, you won't get lost in your triggers. You'll be able to listen to your kids begging you for ice cream and not snap at them. You'll forgive yourself for all the times in the past you've made their desires wrong. You'll finally see why you got so pissed at all of that in the first place. You'll let go of the guilt and the misunderstanding that you're responsible for your kid's happiness. And, you'll give them ice cream—or not—as inspired. No drama.

Sure, it takes a decade or two to really be free, but it's so much better than the alternative. (Ask me how I know.)

The key to freedom is on the other side of doing your work

Every feeling you have, from the disappointment you feel in your relationships to the pent-up rage you have for your boss who works you like a dog, is just showing you what's coming up for you to heal.

Your feelings are the key to your freedom. The path to a life you can't even dream of—yet.

Because in order to have peace in your life today, you have to make peace with your past. You have to release the misunderstandings, stories, BS beliefs, trauma, and held emotions you might not even know are there. Otherwise, that shit continues to haunt you.

Your feelings show you the way.

I could've ignored the feelings that started bubbling to the surface once Julia was safe and I finally began to thaw. But that wouldn't have made them go away. It wouldn't have healed the pain and trauma lurking inside.

Every time I suppressed my feelings or ignored them, sooner or

Because of Amy

later they'd end up knocking me on my ass, demanding to be heard like a three-year-old throwing a tantrum in the cereal aisle.

But, when I finally leaned into the nagging discomfort, dissatisfaction, and feeling like I was crawling out of my skin, that's when everything started to change.

Part Three

Truth is Inconvenient When You're Trying to Live a Lie

Underneath everything, all that exists is Truth.

It's what's underneath the societal expectations, the patriarchal bullshit, the story you were told that you have to work harder than everyone else to "earn" your worth, the belief that you can't be happy until everyone around you is happy first (even though they never are).

But if you've spent your entire life hanging onto the lie that your dad wasn't a raging asshole or that your mom didn't teach you to walk on eggshells, you're going to have a hard time letting go of those lies.

Chapter 7
To Be Alive Means You Have Needs

Three and a half months after the girls were born, at a routine check-up, I told my gynecologist that I had to force myself to eat so I could breastfeed Julia.

I told her I was only getting one to three hours of sleep a night—max. And I was running myself ragged spending my days up at the hospital with Julia, trying to manage a household swimming in debt, and carving out time for two little boys who barely got to see their mom.

Not to mention the crushing guilt of it all.

My gynecologist referred me to a psychiatrist and strongly encouraged me to go. I was surprised. With so many things on fire, I didn't even consider my mental health as something that mattered.

When I walked into his office, Dr. Joe, a tall man with gold-rim glasses, welcomed me at the door and shook my hand. He walked to the chair behind his large, wooden desk, gesturing to the ones across from him, inviting me to sit down. I did and he asked me what was going on in my life.

I stared at him blankly, an awkward silence hanging in the air before I said, "I don't share my heart and stories with people who aren't my friends. If you want me to tell you about myself, I at least need to pretend you're my friend. You need to sit over here."

I pointed to the chair beside me.

He tilted his head and stared at me, considering. Then he got up, came around the desk, and pulled out the chair next to mine so we were facing each other.

Finally, I felt safe enough to share my story.

How do you go on when your daughter dies?

I told Dr. Joe that my identical twins were born fifteen weeks premature. That Amy died in my arms at nine days old. That Julia was still in the hospital fighting for her life. That my sons were five and two-and-a-half years old and it broke my heart that their entire worlds had been thrown into chaos.

I told him I was doing the best I could, but it never felt like it was ever enough for my daughter in the hospital fighting for her life or my boys who wanted their mom.

I told him that when I get stressed my stomach shuts down and I don't want to eat. That I had to force myself to eat anyway so I could breastfeed Julia to make sure her tiny body had the best nutrition for her to grow.

I told him how I was on family leave and my primary focus was being with Julia and taking care of the boys as much as possible. That, thankfully, Nathan wasn't as caught up in the deep grief over losing a child as I was at the time so he could keep the household running. I had nothing left to give.

I struggled to get out of bed.

The dread of living without Amy consumed me.

Without the boys and Julia, I'd have no reason to get up. Every day, it took everything in me to peel myself out of bed in the morning. I'd help get my sons ready for daycare and preschool if I could. Nathan would take them and drop them off.

I'd pump my breast milk with the hand pump, shower, choke

down whatever food I could force myself to eat, and go up to the hospital to spend time with Julia.

At supper time, I'd come home, feed and bathe the boys, and hand them off to whoever was watching them that night so Nathan and I could go back up to the hospital.

Though he didn't tolerate the hospital well, we both loved seeing Julia become more stable. We'd kangaroo her on our bare chests, snuggle in, and celebrate her oxygen saturation levels going up from the touch. She loved it as much as we did.

After what felt like no time at all, we'd go back home to relieve the sitter, and I'd often drive back up to spend more time with Julia. I was lucky if I got three hours of sleep a night.

And as much as I was grateful for the time with Julia and the boys, I still felt like I was going through the motions, wading through waist-deep mud tied to an anchor that kept dragging me down. I felt like I could break down sobbing at any moment. And no one knew it.

The doctors and nurses at the hospital would ask me how I was doing "so well." I'd shrug. It's not like I had a choice. I couldn't afford to crumble. I just kept putting one foot in front of the other, hanging on by a thread, doing what needed to be done.

Dr. Joe listened to it all and said, "You're experiencing situational depression."

He told me I was losing myself in the events of my life and wanted to put me on antidepressants to help me function. I'd never heard of situational depression before, but it made sense. I was depressed that my daughter died. However, I refused to take any medication until I was done breastfeeding Julia, which wasn't going to happen until she turned at least six months old.

In the meantime, he gave me the assignment of doing one kind thing for myself every day.

Sure, I can do that. One kind thing a day? How hard can it be?

Extremely hard, it turns out.

After leaving his office, things got uncomfortable real fast. I sat at the kitchen table, pen and grocery list notepad from the junk drawer in hand, trying to come up with a list of kind things I could do for myself.

And I couldn't think of a single one. Not one kind thing jumped out at me. The empty sheet of paper haunted me.

Finally, I came up with three things:

1. Drink my water with a lemon wedge in it
2. Hang out in nature
3. Ride my bike

That's it. That's all I could think of doing for myself. And even though I judged the shit out of myself for only coming up with three things, I was honestly impressed I came up with those.

My future self would come to understand why. When I was a child, Dad was the only one who could take up space in the room. Our wants and needs (beyond being fed and watered) not only didn't matter, they weren't going to be met. So somewhere along the line, I stopped having them. Why bother acknowledging something you're not going to get anyway?

This was the first time in my life someone asked me to take care of myself. It was a stretch exercise, and I hated it.

I felt dumb seeing how out of touch with myself I was.

At my next session with Dr. Joe, I told him how much I hated this process and how uncomfortable it was for me. He was encouraging and kind, helping me unravel all the ways I was taught taking care of myself and considering my own wants and needs meant I was a bad person.

By my fourth visit with him, it still felt like I was just going through the motions, constantly carrying the weight of Amy's death. Julia's journey continued to be a constant roller coaster, the fear for her safety ate away at me. And I still felt guilty all the time for not being able to be more present for my sons, for being on leave from work even though I was the primary breadwinner, for not being able to help Nathan run the household as much as I usually did... the list went on and on.

But I'd finally stopped breastfeeding, so I agreed to try Prozac.

A typical dose is twenty mg, but after a week I was crawling out of my skin. I was watching my world from a foggy distance, unable to feel anything. Dr. Joe suggested I go down to a geriatric dose of 10 mg. It was the sweet spot. Those blockers helped me to get out of bed in the morning without the doom totally devouring me. It was a necessary miracle to be able to function.

Still, I made it my goal to stop taking them as quickly as possible. I wanted to face life without numbing my emotions, so after a few months, Dr. Joe helped me get off of Prozac. Things were settling down, and even though I was still only getting a maximum of three hours of sleep a night between feeding Julia and her monitors going off whenever she threw a lead, I wasn't on the edge of a cliff anymore.

Get comfortable being uncomfortable

Making a list of all the kind things I could do for myself—and seeing how dismal my list was—opened my eyes to how little time and focus I actually spent on my needs. It forced me to look at how disconnected I was from myself—and I didn't even know it.

Sure, I knew I was stuck in survival mode, doing the best I could. I knew I was overwhelmed and dropping balls all over the place. But considering what I was taught and where I came from, of course I didn't know what I wanted or needed.

I'd built my entire adult life on the awful misunderstanding that my wants and needs didn't matter, and now I couldn't unsee it. As painful as it was, Dr. Joe's exercise shined a spotlight on how little I knew myself, let alone had my own back.

I didn't know a new way existed.

Only when I saw all the ways I was throwing myself under the bus, putting everyone else's wants and needs above my own, could I decide what—if any—changes I wanted to make.

Because of Amy

Only when I realized that I wasn't taking care of myself could I see the negative impact that had on everyone in my life, and decide to act differently.

Only when I realized how awful my patterns were, could I break the habit of falling into them no matter how comfortable they'd become.

But holy shit was it hard.

It took more than a decade to unravel these patterns.

I'd been taught to abandon and reject myself at every turn, that it was my job as a woman to make my husband and children happy before I was allowed to be. I was taught: don't talk, don't trust, and don't feel.

In fact, I surprised myself by asking Dr. Joe to sit on the same side of the desk as me. I was used to being punished for asking for what I wanted and praised for doing what anyone else wanted, regardless of how I felt about it.

Yet, here I was asking for *exactly* what I wanted.

And my request to only share personal stories with people I considered my friends had a profound effect on Dr. Joe, too.

In my short time with him, Dr. Joe moved into a new office and surprised me with a small couch and chair set up in the corner by the window. His new desk was much smaller and tucked in on the other side of the room.

Beaming, he said, "I did it because of you."

After I stopped seeing him, I vowed that once I had my shit together, I'd call him up to thank him for guiding me through the hardest thing I've ever faced and even offer to take him out to lunch. His invitation to take care of myself stuck with me for years, and I kept adding to my list. (You know, like only waiting thirty minutes to go to the bathroom after I realized I had to go instead of waiting an hour.)

Three years later, when I called his office to thank him, he was no longer there. I did some digging and found out he'd died by suicide. During the handful of visits I had with him, he told me he was going through a rough divorce and was struggling with not getting to see his son daily.

His darkness consumed him. And yet, he'd helped me through mine.

To be alive means you have needs

But how do you treat your wants and needs as if they matter when you've been taught they don't? When you don't even know making yourself a priority is an option? When you think you need to make everyone else happy before you're allowed to be?

How do you stop abandoning and rejecting yourself when you don't even know you're doing it?

I thought I needed other people to need me or I'd be abandoned and rejected. I thought I had to focus on meeting my partner's, children's, and boss's wants and needs—and that mine didn't matter. I thought it made me a good person to throw myself into work marathons or enable Nathan's creative passion without asking him to contribute financially or be an equal partner. I thought I had to jump through hoops to give my children the things they asked for regardless of how I felt about it or the toll it took on me.

After I so thoroughly lost myself to their wants and needs, I was left with dregs.

And because I was so disconnected from myself, no matter what I did, it was never enough. My ego would constantly add to the list of what else I needed to do before I was allowed to feel like I was enough or lovable.

I'd tell Nathan I was okay with whatever he was doing, but then I'd be butt-hurt, shut down, and/or punish him with silence—all because I was feeling abandoned and rejected.

I'd tell myself that, if he were a good partner, he'd be able to read my mind. That I shouldn't have to tell him what I wanted or needed —he should just know. Never mind that I didn't know how I felt or why. *He* should. And he should be able to fix it too.

Talk about a setup for pain and struggle, when really, I needed to be ok with my own wants and needs.

Eventually, as I started doing my work, I learned that I could be a good person, with a kind heart, *and* see and meet my needs. I learned I could say 'no' to others. And as annoying as it was, I realized I'd been lying to myself for years by pretending my needs didn't exist.

In Truth, having wants and needs isn't the same thing as "being needy." Pretending you don't need food, water, sleep, Love, emotional connection, or to go pee doesn't mean you don't.

People pleasing won't make you happy when it comes at the expense of losing yourself. Because if your needs aren't being met, you'll recklessly project that pain onto yourself and others, expressing your unhappiness in passive-aggressive, aggressive-aggressive, or even self-abusive ways. It's way more efficient to get intimate with yourself than to keep playing out the disconnect and denying your humanity.

And, when you stop waiting for other people to "make you happy" or "fulfill your needs," you no longer have to resent them or make them wrong for not living up to the fantasy of who you want them to be.

That's freedom. It's having someone ask you for something and not automatically throwing yourself under the bus to be their answer. Or, it's asking someone else for what you want and not getting pissed when they tell you 'no.'

Put simply, self-knowledge is self-Love—and self-Love extends to others.

A growing restlessness

Julia came home on Thanksgiving Day at four-and-a-half months old, weighing in at five pounds, two ounces.

I was so grateful to finally have her home. Her smile lit up my entire day and melted my heart. But having her home tossed our household into a new level of uncertainty and upheaval.

Would she be ok without the 24-hour care from the doctors and nurses? Could I give her everything she needed?

Because she was so little and went through her food quickly, she needed to be fed every two hours—even during the middle of the night. And since her lungs weren't fully developed, she needed breathing treatments and constant monitoring for the first two years of her life.

In those first months at home, before we'd tuck her in, we'd attach leads from her breathing monitor to the fragile skin on her tummy. When she moved the tiniest bit, the leads would detach, setting off the shrieking alarms. Panicked, I'd hit the floor running, rush to her room, heart pounding, and thankfully always find Julia alive, needing comfort from the shrill noise.

At a year old, she got a respiratory virus (RSV) and ended up back in the hospital for a few days. But by the time Julia turned two, she was finally stable enough that I was no longer on a knife's edge, worrying for her safety, stuck in survival mode, barely hanging on. I could take a deep breath.

And while I thought that's when things would get better, that's when the real work began.

Chapter 8
The Gift of Pain

When Julia was five years old, our whole family went to a local Arts Festival in downtown Des Moines, Iowa. As we wandered around, I ran into Dr. Bhavsar, the NICU doctor who first stabilized Amy when she was born.

We shared a hug. He was excited to see Julia and how far she'd come.

Remembering the rollercoaster of emotions in the NICU as Julia fought for her life for over four months, I blurted, "Being in the NICU every day with babies dying, struggling to live, coming back from death's door is hard. What keeps you going day after day?"

My question took him off guard. He paused to think about it before looking over to Julia. Pointing at her, he said, "That's why I do what I do. It's the successes."

His words shook me to my core and I had no idea why.

For the next day and a half, I sat with the agitation I felt when Dr. Bhavsar innocently called Julia's life a success. I kept asking myself why I was so on edge. *Why was I so upset?*

And finally, it hit me. Calling Julia a success implied Amy was a failure—and she wasn't.

Amy's life was full and complete exactly as it was. Most anyone who interacted with her during her nine short days would say the same. I saw how deeply she impacted so many people, and it was unfathomable to me to even remotely insinuate her life had been a failure.

I was reeling because *every* life a doctor touches is a success— even the ones who don't survive.

Amy's life—*and death*—gave me the greatest gift I'd ever received. Just because it came wrapped in pain didn't make it any less valuable, real, or important.

Amy was every bit as much of a success as Julia.

Give yourself permission to face the pain

Before the girls were born, I bought a second-hand stroller that was super wide so both girls could sit side-by-side facing the front.

Other strollers blocked one baby's view, and I didn't want to choose which daughter wouldn't get to see the world. So, even though it was expensive, I had to have it. I didn't care that it would take up more space and make getting through crowds even more challenging.

After Amy died, Nathan hung the stroller in the garage where it sat for months—and months. I couldn't bear the thought of giving it up. The stroller represented an investment in my dreams.

But every time I saw it, I felt a pang of sadness for never having gotten to use it. After the bruises on my ribs faded, I'd look at the stroller on my way out the door or back home from work to remind myself Amy was real.

One day, I pulled into the garage and it was gone.

Nathan had a penchant for giving away things he didn't want around, even if they weren't his. He didn't ask, he just donated or threw things out with reckless abandon. And even though he knew I wasn't ready to let it go, he gave it away.

In shock and disbelief, I flew upstairs and asked him where it was. He went on a rampage, listing all the reasons I was wrong for wanting to keep it. "We don't need it. We weren't using it. It took up space..." anything to defend his position and prove himself right.

I bawled. But it wasn't really about the stroller.

With Julia stabilized and safe, space finally opened up for me to process the unmet feelings and emotions that were kicking my ass. The irritation and restlessness were getting louder and louder. And I couldn't ignore the crushing pain anymore.

Nathan had ripped the Band-Aid off a gaping wound.

His controlling, asshole behavior, the same shit I'd grown up with from my father, was telling me it was time to meet the pain head-on.

So I checked myself into a local hotel room for a weekend to make space for the emotions, restlessness, pain, and grief consuming me without having to juggle the needs of three kids at the same time.

Nathan fully supported the idea. He was relieved to not have me and my big feelings around for a couple of days.

The room came with a loft bed surrounded by windows I could stare out of, a fireplace, and a kitchen—complete with a microwave, stovetop, full-sized fridge, and all the pots, pans, plates, and silverware I'd need to stay tucked in for the weekend.

Friday evening, I built a mesmerizing fire with the paper logs the hotel supplied and stared at it for hours, slowly making space for the grief and confusion I'd kept at bay for so long. I didn't push them away or make them wrong. I didn't try to change them. I felt the emotions underneath my restlessness and irritation come to the surface, letting the discomfort wash through me.

By Saturday, everything felt loud and raw.

After I woke up, I lounged in bed reading *Hannah's Gift— Lessons from a Fully Lived Life* by Maria Housdan. Maria's daughter, Hannah, a little girl with a zest for life, had died of cancer at three years old. Dr. Teri Wahlig, Julia's doctor from the NICU, had gotten the book for me as a gift. I'd been reading it off and on for a while, but in the hotel, I couldn't put it down.

I used Hannah's mother's raw pain to plunge into my own.

I finished the book while soaking in the tub that evening. I sobbed for hours, adding hot water whenever it got cold.

Processing Amy's death felt like facing my own... and it was.

I faced the death of my hopes and dreams. I faced the death of Julia and Amy growing up together with their brothers. I faced the death of my life as I thought it would be.

I was crushed.

I knew I was connected to Amy. I knew she'd always be with me as I held her in my heart. But, I still ached for her presence, still clung to hopes and dreams I'd buried with her. And all those unprocessed feelings haunted me.

Sinking into the water and depths of untouched grief and sorrow, the floodgates opened up to pain, heartache, loss, and torment. My skin pruned over, my heart broke completely open, and I surrendered to it all—lost and confused, wanting answers without even knowing the questions.

I tried to make sense of what it all meant. I wanted to make sense of Amy's death, to give her life meaning.

After wrestling with it, asking non-stop questions to try and figure it all out, I finally gave up the fight. And in the silence, I heard my daughter Amy's voiceless voice of wisdom.

"My life—and my death—are an invitation for you to show the fuck up and live"

On Sunday morning, in the upstairs loft, while packing up my stuff, I paused and laid on my stomach with my elbows propped up and my legs in the air. I stared out the windows.

I had an emotional hangover and no idea what came next. I was empty. All I knew was that Amy's death broke my heart wide open.

I'd be doing laundry for the children, and instead of feeling over-whelmed by the piles and piles of dirty clothes, I was grateful—even seeing the grass stains, stretched-out necklines, and holey knees.

During the sleepless nights when Julia wouldn't stop crying from teething, an ear infection, or nightmares, exhausted as I was, I celebrated her tears.

The challenge of getting three children out the door, piling into the grocery store, shopping, and keeping track of them, was an absolute blessing.

All of it reminded me that my children were alive.

Through the contrast, Amy's death taught me what mattered—and what didn't. Her life shook me to my core. It changed me forever. Both her life and her death gave *my life* meaning.

Only after my heart had been crushed to smithereens did I realize that I wanted more for myself. I wanted to face pain from my past so I could heal. I wanted to live with an open heart no matter what anyone around me said or did. I wanted to stop listening to what everyone told me I should care about and figure it out for myself.

Eventually, I shared this with Dr. Bhavsar, Dr. Wahlig, and Dr. Sahu, the incredible doctors who cared for the girls in the NICU. I wrote them a letter (which was later published in the medical-trade journal *The Neonatal Intensive Care Magazine**) expressing my belief that every soul is a gift to each of us, no matter how long or short they live.

Perhaps their soul was there to show their parents how to cherish life in a way they never could before. Perhaps they showed up to let us know that, even in our isolation, we're never truly alone. No matter what, the success of a child's life is always there—whether they live or die.

Either way, it's all perfection.

The gift of pain

Whether you know it or not, your life is the perfect life for you to learn, expand, and grow.

---

* See Appendix to read the full article

As you're tested—mentally, emotionally, physically, and spiritually—you're being given the opportunity to change. Yes, at times those tests are painful. Your life can be absolutely crushing, devastating, and heartbreaking.

But you learn through contrast.

And while focusing solely on the pain feels like shit, ignoring it doesn't make the pain go away. Denial doesn't change reality. Time doesn't heal all wounds. Only leaning in and doing your work to heal your past will get you where you want to go.

Doing your work is a choice. It requires a willingness to get uncomfortable and to face your fears—even when it feels impossible. Unfortunately, it's often only when your pain is louder than your fear of change that you're motivated to make that choice.

That's why pain is a gift. Because on the other side of facing it, you'll be reborn.

You'll come out with a strength you didn't know you were capable of. You'll have a map and compass to guide you toward Love and Truth—even when the next layer hits.

You just have to face the fog of confusion, loss of self, and heightened emotions first.

More often than not, that's how "doing your work" works. Whenever you're restless, irritated, or feeling out of sorts, you're being shown what's coming up for you to heal. And, there's a ninety-five percent chance that whatever it is will keep showing up again and again, getting louder and louder, smacking you in the face, until you process the held pain so you can finally have peace.

Either way, you get to decide how to respond. You can be grateful for the gifts of pain, dig into them, and use them to heal and grow. Or, you can keep kicking the can down the road to deal with another day.

As an energy healer and intuitive guide I've supported people all across that spectrum. Some people lean in and do just enough to take the edge off, coming back only when their pain is once again raging. Others see the ginormous value of consistently leaning in to find and release their blocks instead of waiting until they're triggered and crawling out of their skin.

For me, once I experienced the freedom and empowerment this work gave me, I was all in. There was no other way.

Pain is a gift—what will you do with it?

I still miss Amy's physical presence. I always will.

But in her physical absence, Amy continues to share gifts with me that are just as significant as the ones from my other children. She's a touchstone that keeps my heart flowing ever so freely.

Processing the trauma of losing a child (not to mention the fear of her sister almost dying and the guilt of not being 100 percent available for my boys during it all), ultimately gave my life meaning.

Because of Amy, I could no longer see life in the same limited ways I had before.

And even though I continued to stay small and not have a voice for years, because of Amy, *staying* stuck was no longer an option.

She changed me forever. Amy's life and death took me to a level of acceptance and surrender I didn't know was possible. Because once I saw her life as whole and complete, I could no longer make anything that happens in life wrong.

Amy's death became a guiding star to what really mattered. Things like a spotless home, panicking when my clients didn't get their overnight reports, or missing some made-up deadline at work (that was impossible to begin with) didn't matter. At all.

As time went on, I could no longer give myself a hall pass for settling, for being afraid, or for holding back because things were hard or emotions were rough.

My daughter handed me the meaning of life: to show the fuck up and really live. Everything except Love and Truth fell away.

Her death was the most painful thing I've ever experienced. And it was an absolutely breathtaking, endlessly precious gift.

Chapter 9
Personal Responsibility is Personal Empowerment

Six months after the girls were born, I went back to work. I'd been chewed up and spit out, completely transformed though no one knew it. A major divide within my team showed me just how much I'd changed.

Even before I went on leave, our IT department was constantly growing and changing. Cubicles shifted, offices shuffled, and equipment moved around. I returned to find everyone on my team up in arms, completely split about where to put the photocopier.

"It's more logical to have it by the computer room."

"No, it makes way more sense to have it at the end of the aisle by most of the team."

As a managing supervisor, the old me, the one before Amy died, would go into a tailspin trying to make everyone happy—and feel horrible when I couldn't.

But having Amy die in my arms changed me.

Now, I clearly saw that everyone *thought* they cared about where the photocopier went. Those extra fifty steps felt like a big deal.

In reality, they didn't give a shit. But they didn't know it because they hadn't just buried their daughter.

During the team meeting, I listened to their arguments about which place was best and why. I told them how much I appreciated that they cared and that no one was wrong for wanting what they wanted.

Then I said, "We're going to go ahead and have it here because the wiring makes the most sense. Walking extra steps may not be your favorite thing, but it's going to be ok. If we need to move it later, we will."

Everyone matched my calm. They knew I cared about them. They all felt heard enough to honor my decision. And they never mentioned it again. It just became their new normal.

My daughter dying was an instantaneous reset to no longer play in the drama. I could finally see how, in our humanity, we make shit up to be upset about without even knowing it.

Doing your work is a process

I want to say that Amy died and I was immediately different. And in many ways, I was.

Losing Amy made falling into my old patterns uncomfortable at best, and excruciatingly painful at worst. But it also took decades of leaning into my feelings and doing my work to really change. It wasn't a one-and-done kind of thing.

Over time, Amy showed me all the ways I lost myself trying to prove my worth, manipulating other people into liking me so I wouldn't be abandoned and rejected, and giving until it hurt and then giving some more so I could "earn" their love.

She helped me *eventually* hop off the hamster wheel, stop chasing these painful motivations, and take my power back. Her death triggered a deep, internal death of my own. She showed me the things that really mattered (Love and Truth).

But I still carried so many bullshit identities and patterns I thought I needed. And unraveling those lies was a process. I still had to face a bajillion more internal deaths.

When my children were eleven, eight, and six, I was once again super restless and didn't quite know why.

I worked forty-sixty plus hours a week, maintained our household, and constantly drove the kids to and from one practice to the next, attended recitals, and walked the dog (all while actively ignoring taking care of myself). But when I wasn't losing myself in work or taking care of the kids, I was miserable. I wanted things to be different but I had no idea where to start.

I'd spent my life worried sick over not being able to meet unrealistic work deadlines or doing whatever I could to keep my dad (and later, Nathan) from getting angry. Falling into people pleasing was second nature. Hell, I even believed that if I ever laughed again, people would think I didn't love my daughter who died.

I told anyone who asked that I was happy. Happy at home. Happy at work. Happily married.

And I was. But I also wasn't.

I didn't feel loved, valued, or respected by Nathan. I just thought that that's what love was. It was exactly like my parent's relationship —and it certainly wasn't happy.

Even when I worked boatloads of overtime, Nathan didn't appreciate me. He wasn't emotionally supportive. He contributed enough to keep the household running, but his bitterness, anger, and resentment sucked the life out of the entire family.

Now the lies were catching up to me, the irritation and restlessness getting so loud that I couldn't ignore them anymore.

Then one day, out of nowhere, I thought, *What if I left?*

Terrified, I pushed the thought away. But week after week, month after month, it kept coming back.

It haunted me.

What kind of mother would consider leaving her kids? You're a horrible person. What's wrong with you? There has to be something else you can do.

Back and forth, the battle raged.

Desperate for any solution that didn't involve facing my greatest fear, I felt like a prisoner trapped in someone else's life. I didn't want to think about leaving my kids. But in all the time I spent judging the hell out of myself for even pretending to consider leaving, I hadn't been able to come up with anything else.

Until one afternoon, something snapped. My heart broke, and I gave myself permission to leave.

At first, self-judgment consumed me. *You're a horrible mother. How dare you consider leaving? The kids would be crushed.*

But I sat with the attacks until I settled into the thought: *Just try it on. What if I left? What would my life be like?*

I thought about leaving Nathan and finding somewhere new to live. It was scary because I'd never done it before, but I knew I'd be more than okay without him.

Then I thought about leaving my children and every cell of my body screamed, "NO."

My kids meant the world to me. I Loved them so much that the thought of living without them on the daily felt like the sun going out. I couldn't bear it.

Still, I couldn't fully appreciate that until I gave myself permission to get real. Until I surrendered the rigid, bullshit story shaped by a judgmental society that said a *good* mother wouldn't even consider leaving.

Once I did, I took the deepest breath I'd taken in months. I had my answer.

From then on, I no longer felt like a victim of my life. I chose to be there. My home was exactly where I wanted to be.

I celebrated my time with my children with a lightness I hadn't been able to experience before. I went out of my way to be available for them. Not just for them, but for myself. Because they were so important to me.

I'd always been taught that taking care of others and making sure they were happy would make me happy. It didn't. But until I faced the fear of being a bad mom, leaving my family, and naming how I really felt, I stayed stuck in pain.

Because fear is like the monster under your bed. It haunts you until you turn on the light, take a look for yourself, and see there's nothing really there.

Healing happens in layers

When I started nude modeling it was a way to connect with Nathan. But it became so much more.

Nude modeling brought me face to face with shame. It helped me to accept my body exactly as it is—A-cups, stretch marks, and all.

But healing happens in layers.

One time I was on the phone with my Mom and she asked if I had any plans for the evening. I told her I was going to model at the art center. After asking more questions and finding out I was modeling nude, she exploded.

I tried to explain to her about how I carried shame about my body and wanted to have a new experience Loving, appreciating, and accepting myself exactly as I am.

She couldn't hear any of it.

Over the next few weeks, she demanded I stop modeling. She even offered to pay me whatever the art center was paying me so I'd stop. I told her it wasn't about the money, it was about releasing the body shame I carried.

Mom went so far as to call Nathan. She begged and pleaded with him to make me stop. It didn't work. He was the one who asked me to do it in the first place.

During one heated conversation, Mom told me that if I kept modeling, I'd end up like Marilyn Monroe, on drugs and dying of an overdose.

At the time, she was my greatest level of support. Even as emotionally shut down and suppressed as she was, she was the only one who gave me compassion. I desperately wanted her to accept me.

But she couldn't. "No child of mine is going to be a nude model. If you keep doing this, you're no longer my daughter."

I was devastated. I sobbed and sobbed, terrified at the thought of losing her. She didn't get it. She didn't see me. She didn't understand. At all.

And she was forcing me to make a choice. I could either be a "good girl" and lose myself to her beliefs and misunderstandings, or I could honor myself. I could keep modeling because it helped me Love, appreciate, and accept my body in a way I'd never thought possible before.

For days, I walked around like a zombie, feeling empty, lost, and disconnected. I finally saw the Truth. My mom wasn't unconditionally supportive. She didn't love me and have my back no matter what.

I cried in the arms of a dear friend as she helped me to grieve the loss of my mom.

Because to do what was right for me, I needed to face my mom's rejection. I needed to face the loss of my person. I needed to see how being the "good girl" to keep my mom in my life came at a steep cost to myself.

When I called my mom back to let her know I was going to keep modeling, for the first time in my life, she hung up on me.

Both of my brothers reached out to me and were super pissed. They weren't angry that I was modeling nude. They were angry that I'd told Mom the truth. One brother even told me that he'd been a nude model in college and that he'd never told Mom. He was pissed I hadn't done the same.

But as hollow as I felt, it was still a relief to have chosen myself. I was tired of hiding so other people would like me. I didn't want their fake approval. I wanted real relationships.

Six weeks after she disowned me, I got a call from my mom.

"Can we make up?" she blurted.

"No. I'm not mad at you, Mom. There's nothing to make up about."

The next time I went to visit her, we were sitting on her patio and I looked into those deep brown eyes that went on forever.

"Mom, the last time you asked me what I was doing, I was honest and told you I was modeling nude at the art center. If you ask me again, and I happen to be modeling, do you want me to tell you or not?"

With a serious yet thoughtful look on her face, she said, "I don't want to know."

"Okay. I want what you want. I'll honor that."

That was a powerful moment for me. I claimed the Truth, and she wanted nothing to do with it. It was a reflection of my childhood: be honest, but not about everything.

I didn't know it at the time, but taking your power back from your parents is a rite of passage into adulthood for everyone. Any relationship where you can't be yourself sucks—including the one with your parents. Walking on eggshells is overrated.

Even after I'd faced abandonment and rejection a bazillion times with my dad, with Nathan, and at work, it was still terrifying to let go of my mom.

On the other side of facing that fear, I was freer. I stood a little taller. I was more me than I'd ever been.

Personal responsibility is personal empowerment

Amy gave me the gift of perspective.

Before she died, I thought so many things mattered that didn't. Afterward, it was clear that no one cares where the fuck you put the copy machine (even if you think you do).

I could see all the ways I focused on things I didn't care about just to be right, to stay stuck, to be the victim, to blame others for abandoning and rejecting me as I blindly abandoned and rejected myself. Amy showed me where I settled for insecurities, littleness, or lack.

And it was unnerving.

I'd fought tooth and nail to keep the disempowerment, misunderstandings, filters, and false beliefs. They were stories I was comfortable with. So when they kept coming up to be healed, they weren't easy to unpack.

Who wants to look at all the shit they've been playing out? Who wants to take responsibility for all the ways they've been contributing to their own struggle?

Uh, turns out, I do. (And whether you know it yet or not, you do too.)

Because when I started getting honest with myself about what I was doing and why, I had the power to change my life.

When I stopped blaming others, I didn't have to wait around for them to change before I could be satisfied and even happy.

When I took responsibility for *my* role in every relationship, I could finally have fun and healthy connections with others—because I knew my own self-worth. I didn't expect them to "make" me feel anything.

But living an empowered life is really hard—and even impossible —until you face old patterns that are keeping you stuck.

Part Four

World Peace Is An Inside Job

This is a world of insanity—and insanity comes from not being aligned with your Soul. It's acting out the pain and blaming everyone and everything else (including yourself) instead of dealing with your core issues. It's hitting your own thumb with a hammer over and over and wondering why you're hurting.

The peace, freedom, and Love you say you want won't come on the other side of your spouse giving up alcohol, your kid marrying the person you think would be best, or losing those last five pounds.

They come when you do the work to heal your pain, your past traumas, and let go of your held emotions, BS stories, and triggers.

Chapter 10
Every Relationship is a Reflection of Your Relationship with Yourself

About a year or two before the girls were born, I loaded up my sons, who were four and one-and-a-half at the time, and went on an adventure to visit my brother and his family in Chicago. On the way there, I swung through my parents' hometown to see them too.

My mom was in the kitchen as I was hanging out with my dad in the living room. Inspired, I called out, asking if she wanted to join us in Chicago. She hemmed and hawed, mulling it over, torn between seeing her family and dealing with a last-minute change of plans. Anything that wasn't planned way ahead of time made her nervous.

I looked at Dad and said, "It'd be nice to have an extra set of hands with the kids."

As if letting me in on some secret, Dad looked at me, nodded, and whispered, "Watch this."

He turned on his best speak-from-the-diaphragm, you-have-to-listen-to-me-because-I'm-a-man voice, and *told* my mom she was going. He shamed and guilted her into accepting my offer, regardless of how she felt.

It wasn't that she didn't want to go. And it wasn't that my dad was making her go because I needed her help or so she could enjoy time with the family. It was to show off to me how much power and control he had.

After Mom went into the bedroom to pack, he shot me a huge grin, tapped me on my thigh, and said, "See!"

In that moment, my dad handed me a huge gift.

For the first time, I saw the manipulation that had played out a bazillion times in my life. He was showing me, with blatant transparency, his controlling asshole ways. With his single, "Watch this," comment, my blindfold fell away. I saw the puppeteer moving and controlling everyone in our household to suit his devious bullshit whims.

As unbelievable, stunning, and shocking as it was, once I saw it, I couldn't unsee it. But knowing better doesn't mean doing better. It took so much processing to unpack the patterns I'd grown up with.

Those patterns and identities were so comfortable they felt like the drive to work I could make with my eyes closed (while also planning out the million and a half other things I had to do that day).

No matter how badly I wanted to make Nathan wrong for his anger and shitty attitude or how badly I wanted to stand up to my dad, I was fighting well-worn habits of being a people pleaser, shutting down, and walking on eggshells.

I was used to recklessly saying 'yes' without asking myself what I wanted. I over-explained everything and apologized for my existence on the daily. And I didn't know I was so uncomfortable disappointing others, that I lost myself along the way. I actually thought I was responsible for their feelings.

Moments like my dad forcing my mom to go to Chicago or struggling to list kind things I could do for myself showed me where I was stuck. They reset my internal compass and interrupted the crazy-making I played out. Over time, I finally began to see that these patterns weren't working.

But unraveling them was like teaching a three-year-old computer programming when they'd never seen a computer before.

It was confusing, messy, and took a lot of trial and error.

I'd seen firsthand that counseling didn't work for my parents. But eventually, I hit the jackpot and found something even more powerful: energy work.

Finding energy work

When my son Thomas was eight years old, he came home from a friend's house after playing football in their basement. His friend's brother smashed into Thomas for a play, and Thomas felt a searing pain in his neck that made him buckle and fall to the ground.

He came home sobbing and in excruciating pain and my maternal instincts kicked in. A gut-wrenching, heartfelt desire to take away my son's pain and help him heal tore through me.

I guided Thomas into the bathroom and took off his sweatshirt. All of a sudden, I found myself looking down at the palms of my hands and I heard a clear "voiceless voice" say, "These hands are healing hands."

I put my hands on Thomas's shoulders and felt a surge of energy blast through my entire body. The energy flowed through me into Thomas. I "saw" clear geometric shapes (triangles, squares, rectangles, etc) enter Thomas's body and bring "light" to his cells. Inside his body, the shapes gathered the pain and injury, turning shades of black and gray before flowing up and out once more.

All of this was an "out of body" experience. I saw myself from the ceiling looking down.

After who knows how much time passed (I think it was minutes but I can't be sure), I knew I needed to take my hands off Thomas's shoulders or I was going to pass out. I didn't know it at the time, but I wasn't "grounded" and because that level of energy or vibration wasn't something I was used to, my knees were buckling.

When I took my hands off Thomas, I not-so-gracefully fell into the bathroom sink and onto the counter. Nathan came home shortly thereafter. And when he did, I told him I needed to get Thomas to the ER.

It was a long drawn-out evening, filled with a shift change, an X-ray, an MRI, and what can only be described as a spiritual experience.

Because Thomas was considered "stable" and a lower priority than another patient clinging to life, Thomas and I had time to tuck into his hospital room together. As each person walked through the door, I would silently explore, "Why are you coming into our life?" Time was non-existent.

Eventually, an X-ray revealed that Thomas's neck was broken. So the doctors prepped me that they'd need to drill metal rods into Thomas's skull to stabilize his head and neck.

I was incredibly present with the process, asking questions, and listening to the answers. Unlike with Amy, I knew everything was going to be okay. No matter what. The whole time, I shared that peace with Thomas and watched in awe at his pure acceptance of what life was offering.

As we waited for the MRI machine to open up so they could have a closer look, Thomas and I searched for Waldo. He couldn't move, of course, so I crawled up onto the table where he was immobilized and laid next to him, holding the book up for both of us to see.

A nurse came in and scolded us, saying it was critical to keep Thomas immobilized. I shared that that was our goal too. I pointed out that nothing about Thomas's current position was compromising that.

With a humph, she said that it would probably be okay as long as we were careful.

Finally, the MRI machine was open and they transported Thomas downstairs. I went with. After the MRI was taken, the radiologist motioned for me to join him in an attached room where he sat in front of a computer monitor with a wall of windows behind it.

He offered me a chair next to him and started showing me images of Thomas's skull and bones. He zoomed into the region of the neck. A couple of minutes passed before he turned to me and with a look of utter surprise said, "I don't even know why I am showing you these."

Immediately I thought, "I know why you are showing me." I knew he didn't have a "choice." I wanted the information. Now. Standard hospital protocol be damned.

He continued. The broken neck from the X-ray was really a growth plate that hadn't completely fused together since Thomas was still growing. His neck wasn't broken after all. His pain was from pulled muscles and tendons.

They hooked Thomas up with a neck brace and sent us home.

I tucked Thomas in after midnight and woke up the next day a completely different person. I was *not* the calm, grounded individual who witnessed this event. I didn't even recognize her.

My mind went into overdrive. "'These hands are healing hands?' *Really*? What *was* that?"

Feeling energies surge through my body, seeing those energies transform, and having an out of body experience as I watched the whole thing from the ceiling, *blew up my world as I knew it*. I knew I'd witnessed a healing for Thomas and that I'd been a conduit for this transformation. But I didn't even consider how a Mother's Love can be such a powerful healing force. I was clueless.

At dinner later that night, I shook with uncertainty at what had taken place. Nathan offered, "Well, Jesus healed people by touching them with his hands, maybe it was like that."

Two weeks later I received emails from friends just hours apart. These friends didn't even know each other. One lived in Texas and the other lived in Utah. But both emails essentially said the same thing... you should look into doing energy work. Reiki.

"Odd," I thought, "Reiki? What's that?" I let it drop.

A month later I went to a workshop with a friend. Turns out thirteen Reiki Masters were there too.

Thirteen? Really? *Really*? Not just one or two but *thirteen*? I went from not even knowing Reiki (energy work) existed to being in a room with thirteen Reiki Masters.

But wait, it gets better. For ten years, they'd all been practicing Reiki, sharing healing energies with each other. One of the Reiki

Masters invited me to join. When she told me where they practiced every Sunday night, my jaw dropped.

They'd been meeting a half a block from my home for the last decade.

The population of Des Moines including its outlying areas is 500,000+ people. And, of all places, they were practicing *that* close to my home? Talk about living your divine life.

After I became a Reiki Master, I was hungry for more. I took classes and tried on all the experiences I could get my hands on. Unlimited Body. Unlimited Breath. Spring Forest Qigong. Jonathan Parker's Quantum Quest School of Enlightenment. Spiritual Response Therapy. Spiritual Restructuring. Breathwork. Sweat Lodges. And more.

Once I found energy work (or perhaps it found me), I began to understand the pain I was in, which helped me to start dealing with it (rather than running away or shutting down). I started to recognize held emotions and misunderstandings that were holding me back. I finally began to see how the traumatic events from my past that I'd never processed had shaped me (and were still kicking my ass).

Suddenly, everything made so much sense.

Using energy work to face my past and heal

People think energy work is woo-woo and way "out there." They're wrong.

Energy work is the most practical, sensible thing there is. It shows you what you're doing and why you're doing it. Like why I couldn't say no to my mother-in-law when she came over and rearranged all my furniture.

Or why I was so desperate for Nathan's attention, I'd settle for any crumb thrown my way and smother him in the process.

Or why I worked hauling bricks with my dad for a full six hours to "prove" my worth to him before telling him I was going to get married.

Every Relationship is a Reflection of Your Relationship with Yourself

Doing my work showed me the Truth of my relationships and the fantasies I desperately wanted to pretend were real. Truth showed me options I didn't know I had, and when I saw the Truth, I could finally consider changing.

It didn't happen overnight and it wasn't any one modality that unlocked everything for me. But over time, I used all my tools to get really honest with myself about why I felt the way I did—and what I needed to do next (if anything).

Every feeling was information, every trigger an invitation to roll up my sleeves and dig in (when I could carve out the time, that is, because I was still a busy mom and wife and the major breadwinner of our family).

But after doing my work, I no longer felt responsible for Nathan's pissy attitude when I wasn't on my A-game acting like super-mom. I no longer had to feel shit-tons of guilt when my kids asked me for something I couldn't (or wouldn't, or didn't want to) give them. And I no longer had to shrink back into my childhood every time I visited my parents.

With energy work, when I was triggered or big feelings came up, I didn't have to shove them down or pretend they weren't there like I'd been taught. I didn't have to make them wrong or shut down. I knew my emotions were just showing me what was coming up for me to heal—and I could use them to dig in and get a shift.

While it took me eleven years to work through major core issues, trauma, and misunderstandings, every time I leaned in to do my work, I fit into my own skin more and more.

I was hooked.

I became a Lover of Truth. I wanted to see everything as it was rather than through the old filters that told me I wasn't lovable or that I had to work harder than everyone else so I wouldn't be abandoned or rejected.

I worked through held trauma and charged emotions until the things that used to trigger the shit out of me no longer felt like being stuck in a tent with a mosquito, but rather like I was watching a fly hit the window trying to get in before giving up and flying away.

And I cleared so much from my past, calling back my energies from the times I lost myself and cutting cords with patterns that didn't serve me, that I became a force for helping others process and clean up the pain from their past too.

I've helped people work through PTSD, sexual abuse, the death of their child or spouse, a complicated relationship with their mother, and the fear of flying, driving over bridges, snakes, and bugs. I helped a client release the pain of a father attacking and trying to kill them, and I've helped many others stuck in childhood dynamics whenever they'd go back home. I created a safe space for their big feelings to come up so they could finally face them and heal.

To this day, it's an absolute honor to have a front-row seat to people making shifts and releasing their feelings of unworthiness, confusion, and held pain.

A Truth you can't unsee

Back in 2007, about nine years into doing my work, I hosted an "Opening Your Heart" workshop for forty-five people.

In preparation, I came across a quote from Eckhart Tolle that left me reeling and blew up all my plans:

 "Relationships do not cause pain and unhappiness, they bring out the pain and unhappiness that is already in you."

As soon as I read it, I knew it was Truth with a capital "T." To say it blew my mind feels inadequate. This quote hit me as viscerally as the meteor that killed the dinosaurs.

I thought I understood unity consciousness and the fact that the outer world reflected my inner one. But it was all in my head—an intellectual experience rather than a true inner knowing.

Every Relationship is a Reflection of Your Relationship with Yourself

When this quote sunk in, I finally knew at every level—mentally, emotionally, and physically—that I was suffering in my relationships *because I was in them.* I could see all the ways I blamed everyone else when, really, I was the problem.

I recklessly abandoned and rejected myself on the daily, all while trying desperately to convince other people not to leave me.

I sought time, attention, approval, and love from most everyone (especially men). I believed the t-shirt my sister got me in high school with two glittery bunnies that said, "You're no bunny 'til some bunny loves you." And let's be clear, if they did love me, I couldn't take it in anyways because I didn't Love myself.

I thought it was my job to regulate other people's emotions and that I was responsible for their feelings. I wanted everyone else to change so *then* I could feel safe, chosen, and happy. Meanwhile, I'd never unpacked how lonely and disconnected I felt, I never saw how I was giving my power away hoping everyone else would be my answer.

I wanted Nathan to see me, love me, value me, and choose me, but I wasn't seeing, Loving, valuing, or choosing myself.

And, now that I saw how my own choices and beliefs kept me held in pain, struggle, limitation, and disconnect, I couldn't do it anymore.

On that blustery March morning of the workshop, I pulled into the hotel parking lot, grabbed my box of goodies to present, and made my way to the entrance.

In the box was a small pink balloon on a plastic stick with the words, "I Love You," written in big, block letters. As soon as I shut my car door, a giant gust of wind caught the balloon and sent it flying.

Dropping the box, I chased the runaway balloon halfway across the parking lot before I finally got it. I burst out laughing at the irony. Once again, here I was, chasing after love, just like I had a bajillion times before.

It was the perfect example to bring into the "Opening Your Heart" workshop.

Eckhart's quote had taken a leaf blower to my house of cards. It showed me that, no matter what anyone else did or didn't do, I was only ever seeing them through my perceptions. My feelings were only ever inside me.

It's no wonder I married an emotionally unavailable man—I was emotionally unavailable to myself.

But now, whenever I was triggered, the person, event, or situation I was triggered by was an absolute gift—even when it was wrapped up in pain (or when they were being an asshole).

That pain was already in me. And if it was mine to begin with, I could do something about it.

Every relationship is a reflection of your relationship with yourself

You don't see things as they are. You see them through your filters of pain and struggle.

So your relationships provide insight into yourself. They reflect back to you your own thoughts, beliefs, feelings, and unresolved emotions.

Unless you unpack the misperceptions, beliefs, and BS lies you may not even know are there, you'll keep attracting relationships and situations that trigger the shit out of you. Even when you leave a relationship, you'll re-create those patterns at work. Or with your children. Or at book club.

Why? Because you're seeing the world through the stories you don't know you're telling yourself or the held emotions you've never dealt with. And the triggers are showing you what's coming up to heal.

When I didn't know how to have my own back, I'd work endless amounts of overtime, which of course was never enough. It was the same at home—I'd add more gardening, cooking, house projects, and children's activities to my plate than I could ever get done.

When I did have downtime, I'd feel guilty I wasn't doing the next thing on the list. And I sucked at relaxing, so I kept doing more and more and more and more...until I'd crash and burn and end up in bed for a day—or three—terrified I'd never have energy again. Then I'd rise up like the phoenix and start the burnout cycle all over again.

The Truth is I felt like I had to "earn" my worth. I believed I needed to work harder than everyone else in every relationship, and then work some more. I didn't think I could take time off because no matter what I did, it was never going to be enough. Until I saw that pattern, I kept replaying it over and over and over again, in all my relationships.

That's the Mirror Universe. It's exactly what Eckhart's quote meant. Your filters, beliefs, held emotions, and the stories you're telling yourself dictate your experience of the world.

When you're triggered or unhappy in a relationship, it's *not* because of the other person (even when they're being an unreasonable asshole).

It's because of you.

That means, the most important relationship that you have is the one you have with yourself.

If your relationship with yourself isn't Loving, kind, healthy, and strong, with clear and clean boundaries, none of your other relationships will be either.

The problem is, you've been taught the exact opposite.

You've been taught to look for a partner who completes you, to give your children everything you never had and live vicariously through them, and to ignore all your wants and needs so everyone at work thinks you're pulling your weight.

You've been expecting everyone around you to be your answer, to give you love, to see you, to make you feel better. And even if they do love you, you can't take it in if—at your core—you don't believe you deserve it.

You're jumping through hoops trying to get everyone else to like you. And you're using their thoughts, feelings, words, and actions as "proof" you are or aren't lovable.

You don't know *you're* the only one who can give yourself what you want and need. You don't know you're waiting to be seen, Loved, valued, and cared for *by yourself*. You don't know it's *your* job to accept yourself.

You don't know you're the one you've been waiting for.

It's counterintuitive, but what if, instead of focusing on everyone else and how they need to change, you took a closer look at yourself?

In our society, we shame everyone for being self-centered, but what if knowing and connecting with yourself isn't about being self-ish? What if connection with yourself is the only way to live authentically?

No one else can meet all your needs. No one else can make you feel safe. And it's no one else's job to see, understand, or Love you. It's yours.

Waiting for them to "make" you feel worthy or lovable is living disconnected from yourself. It will never work. Without knowing who you are, what you want, and what you need, you're fucked (and not in a fun way).

Every relationship is a reflection of your relationship with yourself. So, all your judgments of other people are really your judgments of yourself. If you don't fully accept yourself, you won't be able to accept anyone else.

In other words, a healthy dose of narcissism is the natural state of humanity. It has to be. Like anything else, you can take it to unhealthy levels, but denying the fact that you have wants and needs is just as painful as pretending your wants and needs are the only ones that matter.

Give yourself the gift of personal empowerment

Eckhart's quote finally showed me how everything I was doing as an adult mirrored my experience growing up.

I saw how my mom taught us to walk on eggshells and do

anything we could to please Dad and avoid making him angry. And I saw how I did the exact same thing with Nathan.

Understanding that every relationship was a reflection of my relationship with myself helped me dig deeper into doing my work. It helped me unravel all the patterns I didn't know I was playing out. It enabled me to clear the held emotions, bullshit beliefs, lies, and misunderstandings from my past that were keeping me locked in pain and suffering.

And it ended my constant chase to get other people to love me so that I could feel loved, safe, happy, satisfied, and like I was enough.

It wasn't an easy road. And it certainly wasn't glamorous. But it's been the most rewarding, empowering, Loving, and fun journey I've ever experienced.

When I stopped seeing other people as the problem, I didn't have to wait for Nathan to change. I didn't have to try to convince my children I was lovable. I didn't have to bend myself into a pretzel to please a boss who was only ever going to take advantage of my workaholic tendencies.

I could choose to be happy, right now, no matter what was going on around me.

And life got so much sweeter when I did.

Chapter 11
You Aren't Your Past, But It Does Shape You

Looking back, I can see exactly why my mom and dad were the way they were.

My mom grew up in a household with strong Catholic values. She was taught to be the good girl by being a doormat for her husband and kids.

After they married and had my four older siblings, my mom and dad lived in the country. Isolated and extremely lonely, my mom had her hands full running a household, raising her kids, and dealing with Dad's geyser of control, anger, and rage. You never knew when he would blow.

When a neighbor lady confessed to Mom that she was the one who killed a child in a hit-and-run accident in a local parking lot, it threw my mom into a dark and dangerous tailspin. She carried the burden of knowing what happened while his family and the entire town searched for answers and mourned his death.

She confided in a local priest who told her to keep quiet and not tell anyone. One more time, here she was, being told to shove down her feelings and pretend they weren't there.

Mom suffered a nervous breakdown.

After multiple hospital stays, various treatments, and months of recovery, the doctor said she needed something positive to focus on. He told her she should have another baby, so I was born.

As for my dad, he never bonded with his mother. She was pregnant with him when her eight-year-old son, Emil, died of pneumonia.

His mom was so grief-stricken she refused to even name my dad. She didn't want to love again for fear her heart might be broken beyond repair. Unaware of what had happened, the nurses innocently named my dad Emil, just like his now-dead brother. After some kerfuffle, he was renamed Irvin.

My dad's parents treated him and his younger sister as cheap labor. No matter how much they worked, it was never enough.

Even as an adult, my dad could varnish his mother's log-cabin home, do yard work, and fix her light fixtures, and she wouldn't so much as thank him for it. She was too stuck in the trauma of her own childhood and couldn't get past losing her son.

At fifteen, my dad lied about his age and joined the Army to get away from home. After the Army, he did a stint in the Navy too.

Later on, mutual friends set my parents up on a blind date. They hardly got to see each other while dating because Mom lived in Chicago and Dad lived a couple of hours away. Six months later, they were married anyway.

The night before the wedding, my mom expressed concerns to her parents about my dad's anger. Her parents told her getting married was the right thing to do and, being the good Catholic girl she was, she obeyed.

Even early on, Mom suffered Dad's venomous rage. Once, after my older sister was born, my mom actually left my dad. Her parents told her to go back to him, so, with nowhere else to go, she did.

But, in order to live with him, she had to put her blinders on and pretend things weren't as bad as they were.

She often used my brothers as her counselors, telling them things they were too young to process. When they got (rightfully) pissed at Dad for how he abused Mom and stood up to him, she'd make up with Dad to "keep the peace," unintentionally throwing them under the bus.

Having grown up at the mercy of his mom's abuse, getting off on power plays, controlling others, and pushing them away before they could abandon and reject him was a deeply ingrained survival mechanism for my dad. Meanwhile, my mom let him get away with these power plays because she didn't know how to stand up to the bully (and because of that, when she tried, he just got worse).

I was the only one of five siblings to not get kicked out of the house at least once. Still, being raised by my parents left its mark.

That pain was passed from my parents directly to me (and my siblings). And because I didn't know how to deal with it as it happened, it got stored in my body as trauma until I did my work to unpack it.

To some degree, I re-created the same shit with Nathan and my own kids. It's all I knew.

Trauma is anything you experienced that your body couldn't process when it happened

Your body operates in homeostasis. Meaning, it loves a good normal and will do whatever it can to get back there.

But "normal" is based on what you learned while growing up.

That's why it can be so hard to change your behavior as an adult. Because, even when you know you're "supposed" to drink more water or work out regularly, you're fighting against your comfort zone of being dehydrated and not moving.

You have to actively work to make a change. And that's true for your nervous system, the trauma you've got stored in your body, and what you think love feels like. It's true for the lies you believe, the stories you're telling yourself, the filters through which you see the world, and the patterns you fall back into again and again.

Trauma holds you hostage—and you don't even know it.

I didn't know my dad couldn't be open and Loving to me because he didn't Love himself. I didn't know he lived in a hell realm and projected that pain and struggle onto everyone in our family. I didn't know he regularly lashed out and abandoned and rejected people he supposedly loved as a way of protecting himself from wounds he carried over from his childhood.

I just thought it was normal.

I thought I had a happy childhood. But believing that story meant I had to overlook my dad's overpowering control and explosive anger. It meant putting blinders on to the abuse I experienced. It meant pretending I wasn't sexually assaulted by my brother and then never allowed to speak about it again, and that my mom didn't send me into the lion's den alone to bring my brother food shortly thereafter.

But once I started doing my work, I couldn't keep pretending.

It's not that my entire childhood was shit. But if I wanted a new way, I had to face the lies I'd been taught to uphold. I couldn't just see the happy moments, I had to look at and process the pain and heartbreak I lived through too.

Mom taught us to walk on eggshells to do anything we could to please Dad and avoid making him angry. My dad constantly told all of us kids, "It's my way or the highway. If you don't like it, there's the door." And they both refused to look at any negative emotions closely, to the point where my own father refused to attend my daughter Amy's funeral or acknowledge her death—ever.

And when you've grown up in abuse and you're used to pain, you'll play that shit out again and again. You'll do things exactly like my dad did and scream at your sixteen-year-old daughter on the way to the hospital, blaming *her* for causing your wife's heart attack even though *you're* the one who's just been on a three-day, non-stop rage fest.

When you've been taught love is shutting down when the man throws anger at you, you'll marry an emotionally unavailable angry man so you can "complete" each other. Emotionally available, stable men will feel too safe and too boring. And stepping off the drama roller coaster you're used to will feel absolutely intolerable because you're so used to feeding your pain. (Ask me how I know.)

Until you unpack the held emotions, traumas, misunderstandings, and beliefs you don't even know are there, you'll never really know what Love feels like.

Until you see your past in Truth, both the joy *and* the pain, you'll keep re-creating it over and over again—even when it's with your spouse instead of your parents.

Keep the lesson and let go of the pain

My parents were doing the best they could with where they were and how they were raised. Their best often sucked, but it's all they knew.

And it's all I knew. So I took those lessons into adulthood too.

I married a man with just as much anger as my father, though Nathan didn't outwardly rage in the same way. I lost myself all over the place, at home and at work. I unknowingly taught my kids that men were more important than women, because that's how I showed up in the world. It's what I believed.

Even as a grown-ass woman with a family of my own, I'd go back home to visit my mom and dad and immediately fall back into familiar patterns where Dad was the bully in charge of us all (even when I knew what he was doing).

It wasn't until a few years into doing my work, after the girls were born, but before I read Eckhart's quote, that I finally had a different experience with my dad.

It was a Friday night, and I went to visit my parents for the weekend. I drove three-and-a-half hours to Dubuque, Iowa, children in tow, only for my dad to make some asshole, bullying comment within our first ten minutes there.

I don't even remember exactly what he said and it doesn't matter. He had a way of digging in and degrading you for not making the same choices he would. Or he'd famously pull out his mental list of everything you'd ever done so he could belittle and judge you for it.

Once again, he was throwing shade so he could feel powerful.

And I was done. Done being pummeled. Done watching my dad act like the big man on campus, touting the fifth commandment to "honor your father and your mother" as law to justify his abuse. Done letting him condemn me on a whim. Done pretending he was on some non-existent pedestal.

I looked up at him from my chair and matter-of-factly said, "If you keep this up, I'm leaving right now."

I didn't threaten him. I didn't play into any drama. I just named my Truth from a place of self-empowerment.

And Dad stopped in his tracks. He transformed into Prince Fucking Charming for the rest of the weekend, acting like nothing ever happened.

It was a totally new experience for both of us.

Dad was used to meeting people from a place of power, but he wasn't used to us meeting *him* there. After he made my mom go to Chicago with me, I saw how we kowtowed to him. But when I finally changed the way I showed up, he had no choice but to change. He couldn't play out the family pattern alone.

In a rare moment, I met my dad with an uncompromising clarity of what I needed and wanted in order to have my own back. And it felt good to stand taller.

I knew trying to control him was a fool's game where everyone lost. But it wasn't until I did my work to change my relationship with myself, that I saw my other relationships change right before my eyes.

It's what I'd always wanted but didn't know how to create.

With energy work, I was finding more and more ways to be Loving and authentic to myself. I was no longer willing to throw myself under the bus to placate anyone, including my dad.

For the first time in my life, I didn't need to win his approval or fight for a connection. I didn't take his self-righteousness and anger personally, and I was no longer interested in manipulating him into loving, valuing, or respecting me.

Slowly but surely, I stopped participating in the insanity. Even when I was triggered by something he did or gave him a hall pass for his shitty behavior, I finally had a solid touchpoint of what a new way looked like. And it felt amazing!

You aren't your past, but it does shape you

Wanting your life to change while pretending your past never happened is a recipe for disaster.

In doing my work to unpack why I felt and acted the way I did, I realized that many situations where I was triggered and completely shut down had nothing to do with what was going on around me.

It had everything to do with what I experienced in the past.

Like when Nathan threw his anger and frustrations at me, I'd give him the silent treatment for two to three days at a time. I didn't know it but I was reverting back to my childhood.

I didn't feel safe. At all.

Growing up, we weren't taught how to deal with anger in a healthy way, so I'd never processed it. As an adult, I mishandled Nathan's anger the same way I was taught to avoid dealing with my dad's: by shutting down.

As I leaned in to do my work, I realized the only way to fix my response to anger was to lean into my past. I had to revisit the points of trauma and misunderstandings, and deal with them before I could move forward.

Eventually, I learned that desperately trying to convince people who were hurting me to treat me better, was a sign of my childhood trauma. It made perfect sense why I was hyper-focused on finding a special relationship that made me feel "whole" and Loved.

It made sense that I chose Nathan. Our patterns, filters, and misunderstandings were so perfectly aligned, we would've picked each other whether we were in a crowded room blindfolded or on a season of *Love is Blind*.

And it made sense that I struggled in our relationship. I expected him to be different than he was. I wanted him to make me happy, so my happiness depended on his mood. I was caught in an endless loop that left me depleted, miserable, and trying to control things I couldn't.

Living with the filter that I needed Nathan to complete me was like trying to build a house of cards during a tornado.

Once I saw the Truth, the lie was no longer an option. I had to let the house of cards blow away.

But Truth is revealed in layers. You won't see something until you do. You've been taught to blame everyone else, to set bullshit "boundaries" to justify your rigidity, or to run away from your feelings.

In the first seven years of your life, you came to conclusions based on your environment, your parent's beliefs, and what you were taught culturally. You don't know it, but unless you've done your work, you're still seeing the world through those misunderstandings and bullshit conclusions as if they're real.

Like the child who yearns for his mother to come home, but she's too busy chasing men after her divorce. He'll take her lack of attention and the absence of connection as "proof" he's not lovable, that love *is* the chase.

Then, as an adult, when he meets someone who loves him, unconsciously, he won't believe them or take it in. He'll subconsciously think if he has access to it, it's not love. He'll be so consumed by chasing love in his adult life, he'll only ever choose people who mirror back to him his own feelings of inadequacy. Real Love will be too foreign and too uncomfortable to accept.

But he doesn't have to stay stuck in the chase forever. And neither do you.

Your past doesn't define you, but it does shape you.

And when you do your work to heal your past, you're ultimately healing your entire family as well as yourself. You're healing for your ancestors, your children, their children, and beyond.

Chapter 12
You Teach People How to Treat You

I've always loved the feeling of closeness that sex gave me.

I rarely, if ever, told Nathan no, because those precious minutes of intimacy and feeling chosen before he came and rolled over to go to sleep were all I knew. I was a willing participant with a high libido, even though I didn't have my first orgasm until right before I turned thirty.

Outside the bedroom, he'd draw me with double D's and a tiny waist, distorting my body into a fantasy that looked nothing like me.

But for years, I didn't know Nathan was addicted to pornography.

When I found out, I was devastated. Not only was he spending money we didn't have, but I didn't look like the women in the videos he watched. I didn't sit on the edge of the chair, boobs thrust out with a sultry, "I want to fuck you" look on my face. One more time, it felt like I was being told I wasn't enough.

This isn't a moral judgment of pornography. It's not about vilifying an entire industry. If you're having fun with your fantasy—and you know it's a fantasy—good for you. But Nathan's fantasy looked nothing like women in the real world. It looked nothing like the woman he slept next to every night, the woman desperate to intimately connect with him.

He wasn't wrong for wanting what he wanted. But he couldn't share moments of connection or intimacy with a fantasy.

You can't snuggle or giggle with a woman on a screen. You can't build a life together or raise kids together or sit on a porch swing laughing at your grandchildren together.

His fantasy was an endless chase for something that didn't exist. And it was lonely.

His entire life, he'd been taught sex was wrong. He was raised with Catholic shame and from that oppression an obsession grew. It was way safer to chase the fantasy than to show up and face blocks and limitations to intimacy that he didn't even know were there.

But it was the same for me.

While he fantasized about a woman that didn't exist, I fantasized about a relationship with my husband that wasn't real. I wanted to have an emotional connection with Nathan, but he was emotionally unavailable. And all the while I was, unknowingly, emotionally unavailable to myself—or him. That's why I picked him.

I didn't know it, but Nathan didn't make me feel inadequate by obsessing over pornography. He simply showed me all the ways I already felt inadequate as a woman. He showed me my deepest insecurities—and they had nothing to do with him. They were already inside of me.

I wanted to feel chosen. I wanted to feel like I mattered. And I didn't. But it wasn't about him.

To me, his obsession meant something was wrong with me. If he was looking for satisfaction elsewhere, it must mean I wasn't enough of a woman for him. I didn't know I was the one who felt that way about myself.

Even after finding out he was into porn, I had no idea what to do about it.

My Catholic upbringing taught me divorce wasn't an option. And I was terrified of being alone. So, I tried to accept and understand Nathan despite my insecurities and despite feeling like I was crawling out of my skin every time he chose to be alone in his studio instead of hanging out with me and the kids.

I'd listen to him share his love for the female body and desire to break through the shame of his upbringing. And measure that against all the ways he told me I wasn't enough.

Once, he even asked me to get breast implants.

To this day, I Love my response: "NO, it would ruin my golf game."

I don't play golf. I was repulsed at the thought of putting anything foreign in my body. Still, I wanted to please him so I settled for gel inserts in my bra.

If you want your relationships to work, you have to deal with your past

Being married to Nathan felt both familiar and different at the same time. Even though he didn't rage outwardly like my dad, Nathan was still a very angry man. But Nathan's anger felt natural, like crawling into your own bed after a long vacation away (sure it's lumpy and you forgot to change the sheets before you left, but it's familiar).

Like my dad, Nathan was opinionated and forced his beliefs onto the world and everyone in it. He played out exactly what his dad taught him, thinking that throwing his anger around would make the people or situations he was angry at change. It didn't, but this belief consumed him. He brought his anger to his family of origin, me as his wife, his children, politics, and to all of his disappointments in life.

But I had no idea I deserved to be treated any better.

I was clueless that I was the problem—that I'd re-created my childhood normal by marrying an emotionally unavailable, angry man and desperately vying for his acceptance. Even when I did get a nod of approval from Nathan, it was never enough. With Nathan's "support," I felt abandoned and rejected over and over again, whether he was buying me flowers or exploding in anger.

I had no idea that while desperately seeking his approval, I was abandoning and rejecting myself all over the place. I wanted him to choose, love, and accept me, but I wasn't remotely doing any of those things for myself. I was an emotionally unavailable asshole to myself and I didn't know there was another way.

As I did my work, I figured out that my marriage was a reflection of how I felt about myself and what I thought I deserved. That realization gave me a blueprint to follow. I finally had something I could change and control. And it was *me*.

I started to take responsibility for my triggers. They meant something was up for me to heal. Knowing I wasn't the victim of what anyone else said or did was like opening the doors of my own personal jail cell (and realizing they were unlocked the entire time).

I didn't have to get butt-hurt that Nathan chose porn over me. I could unpack my own insecurities and body shame.

I didn't have to blame my boss for asking me to work sixty-plus hours a week meeting every unrealistic deadline. I could see all the ways I thought I needed to "earn" my worth and start to give myself the Love I craved from others. I could give myself the grace to say 'no.'

I didn't have to worry about my children abandoning and rejecting me. I could stop abandoning and rejecting myself and learn to Love them no matter how they felt about me.

Once I saw the patterns for what they were and how they limited me, I could stop playing them out ad nauseam.

And that awareness was essential to my growth. It was the connection and true intimacy I'd always wanted.

That's when I let go of my desperate urge to look for love and approval from everyone else. That's when all my close relationships either blossomed or fell apart. And it's when I finally created a life I Love.

But, it took time and effort

Even after I started to do my work, there were times I still felt crushed by the actions (or inactions) of others. They were innocent and just being themselves, but unpacking my core issues of abandonment and rejection (issues I didn't even know were there) meant life got messy.

Every time I faced a new layer, I was terrified I'd end up alone.

Unknowingly, I was fighting my ego, the part of me that didn't feel safe when other people loved me. The part of me that would add to the never-ending list of things I needed to do to "earn" love—and the parts that didn't believe I deserved it.

From that place, I was never going to feel safe. I was going to keep looking for all the ways people were going to abandon and reject me —and since that's what I was looking for, it's what I found.

I was completely innocent. Then again, so was Nathan. We only knew what we knew. But those patterns ran deep.

I'd tell him, "I love you," every single day. I wanted him to do the same because Nathan telling me he loved me helped me feel safe, chosen, and secure, something I hadn't known as a child.

Rather than healing the part of me who didn't know I didn't feel lovable, I wanted him to fill that void for me.

But he'd say he loved me back once every six months or so.

It frustrated me to no end. In the second year of our marriage, I finally blew up. Sobbing, I asked him why he didn't tell me he loved me more often. He had an explanation...and I hated it.

"When I tell you I love you, you jump for joy and get so excited. I love that. I don't want it to get old, so I don't want to say it too much."

I wanted to drink from the fountain of Love every day. He wanted to go there for special occasions so I'd react like someone who just stumbled on an oasis after wandering around the desert with an empty canteen.

After that, I told him I never wanted to be without the pool, I wanted to swim in the abundance of Love every day. I wanted a new experience, for him to know my heart.

And, for a while, he did tell me he loved me more often. But eventually, that too stopped.

Having a new experience wasn't about asking him to change. It was about seeing, facing, and letting go of all the ways I abandoned and rejected myself. Because Nathan telling me he loved me was like throwing pennies into quicksand hoping to fill the hole. There were never going to be enough pennies.

You teach people how to treat you

Early on, Nathan would buy me flowers.

Innocently, I'd shrink in fear, feeling guilty over how much money he spent on these high-end, boutique arrangements. So much so I couldn't even fully enjoy the flowers. And I *love* flowers.

I'd tell him, "You shouldn't spend money on this." And eventually, he didn't. He stopped buying me flowers, or anything else, really.

Simultaneously, he'd buy whatever he wanted for himself without telling me (even when I was the only one earning money and credit card debt was consuming us).

I'd taught him not to bother with getting me nice things and to let whatever he bought go unmentioned. We weren't partners, and it was every bit as painful as it sounds.

Unconsciously, I'd taught Nathan (and everyone else around me) that I wasn't worthy. And even if they did see me as worthy, I couldn't take it in because it wasn't what I believed about myself.

When I finally saw the Truth, I watched in real-time how I'd taught my children the very same lessons I'd choked down as a kid.

I saw them play the "dad's the most important" card, scrambling to be with him and doing whatever it took to get his attention and approval. My time and attention weren't perceived as valuable to them. Why? Because, for the most part, I made myself available to them. I taught them they could rely on me and come to me no matter what.

I taught them that my attention and approval could be taken for granted (which is healthy). But I also taught them that their dad's attention and approval were precious. They had to be earned.

As an adult, you've taught people how to treat you too.

How you responded to their words, actions, and inactions was all a part of showing them what you thought you deserved. You shut down and froze, threw up walls, reacted to their disrespect by lashing out, or tolerated their abuse, often pretending it wasn't there or didn't matter.

Or you played the asshole bully to everyone else because you were too scared to be vulnerable and didn't know any other way.

You've created your world based on the stories, misunderstandings, filters, traumas, and triggers you don't even know you're carrying.

Breaking patterns isn't easy. You'll reach for your comfort zone automatically, even if it feels like shit—because it's what you're used to.

So, when you say you want more love, happiness, peace, joy, and freedom, if you're putting up with a boss who demands you work sixty hours a week, a partner who won't talk to you about anything that matters, or children who take advantage of your kind heart, chances are you've taught them through your repeated behavior that that's what you expect and deserve.

It's no one else's job to see, understand, or know you. They don't have to change for you. They get to ask you for whatever they want. And you get to decide how to respond. You're the creator.

And the only way out of relationship dynamics you hate is to start honestly looking at yourself.

Where are you projecting blame onto other people and situations, punishing them instead of realizing you're the problem?

How are you talking to yourself in your head? Is it the kind, loving talk you'd want from a best friend, or do you beat yourself up on the daily?

What are you hanging onto even though it's been twenty-plus years? What are you still bitter, angry, and resentful about?

Are you really leaving the relationship, job, or country because it's the right thing to do, or is it because you're avoiding your feelings (and will therefore re-create those feelings again and again and again and again)?

Awareness of what you've done in the past—and why—is the first step to self-realization. Without that, you'll keep playing out your shit and losing yourself all over the place.

Because if you're used to relationships where you feel abandoned and rejected, those people don't need to change. You need to heal your relationship with yourself. You need to see, face, and heal all the ways you abandon and reject yourself first.

Otherwise, you'll keep teaching others to treat you the same way, whether it's with a new partner, your kids, your job, or the TSA agents checking your bags at the airport.

The Truth is a healing balm

Four years before we divorced, Nathan and I went to a marriage counselor. By that point, he refused to talk to me about any topic except the children unless we were sitting on opposite ends of a couch in front of our counselor.

I wanted to be happily married. I wasn't. I was repeating my childhood pattern of trying to please my dad by losing myself. But I was willing to work on our marriage.

During one of our four sessions, the counselor asked Nathan if he wanted to stay married to me. He said he did.

"Are you fucking kidding me?"

I hit him with all the ways he wasn't showing up, wasn't talking to me about anything except the kids, and all the ways he treated me poorly.

Everything he did told me he was done with our marriage.

I got in his face, challenging him again and again. Every time he came back with some weak-ass attempt to convince me he wanted to stay, I'd blast him with all the ways he showed me it wasn't true.

Finally, exasperated, he blurted out, "I've wanted a divorce for the last three years!"

Relief washed through my body as all the years of confusion fell away. Even before he'd admitted it, his actions had been loud and clear. The lies and pretending were downright exhausting and hurtful to both of us.

He was afraid if I knew how he felt, I'd pull the plug on the marriage immediately, and he wasn't financially ready to support himself. But now that we knew the Truth, we could figure out how to disentangle, become independent, move forward, and heal.

We didn't need to go back to the counselor. We had our answer.

After that last session, Nathan still wanted to be in my bed.

"No. I deserve one room in this house where I can close a door, just like everyone else, including you. You can put a bed in your studio downstairs. We're done."

I wasn't going to let him continue to hold me, snuggle with me, and then refuse to talk with me like we'd been playing out for months.

That behavior was confusing, and I was done being treated that way.

Later on, Nathan even got angry at me for taking the shit and abuse he'd dealt me over the years and for not standing up for myself. He was right. In rare moments I would stand up to him, but I never fully met the bully. I didn't know how.

Now we had to figure out how to move forward knowing we were getting divorced. With one kid at home and two in college, we wanted to disentangle our marriage in the best way possible for our children, our finances, and ourselves. We wanted to be responsible and do it with kindness.

And that meant facing even more fears I didn't know were there.

Part Five

Doing My Work Gave Me My Life

Leaning into the pain from your past and taking an honest inventory of what you're doing—and why—is some of the hardest work you'll ever do.

There's a reason most people want to "move on" like it never happened, sweep things under the rug and never talk about them again, or convince themselves they're fine.

And they're not wrong for doing so.

But on the other side of doing your work is a life you've always dreamed of. One that doesn't come from your latest promotion, same-day delivery package, relationship, or luxury vacation.

Doing my work quelled the restlessness, irritation, aching, despair, and desperation I felt while searching for happiness outside of myself.

It helped me make sense of why I constantly drove myself into the ground around the holidays to make sure everything was "perfect" or chose an emotionally unavailable man who couldn't see, love, or truly appreciate me.

It freed me from chasing after him and my children to love me.

It took me more than a decade to get clear, but the more I did my work, the more connected, alive, and free I was. The more space I had to be me. The more I felt Loved, valued, and respected (regardless of what anyone else said or did).

That's what's available to you too, if you're courageous enough to lean in.

Chapter 13
Happiness is a Choice

Nathan's anger was hard to live with, but it's what I was used to. Each morning for twenty-seven years he put on his pissy pants, bitching about politics, the economy, his family of origin, his former boss, or where the neighbor parked their car—all to justify his attitude.

At first, it felt like us against the world.

But over time, especially after his mom died, he started hurling the anger he had for her (and everything else) onto me.

I finally saw him for the piranha he always was. But now, instead of being safely on the outside, watching as he tore into someone else's flesh, I became the bait he was after, trapped inside a tiny tank with him and those razor-sharp teeth.

He used anything I did to justify his anger.

I shouldn't prefer veggies and salads over meat and potatoes. I shouldn't spend months painstakingly planning and bringing to life home improvements he didn't care about. I shouldn't ask for his input on how to furnish or decorate our home.

I was wrong for being cold when he turned on the AC in the summer, for wanting to spend time together as a family, for being careful with our money, and for getting sick, burned out, or not being Supermom.

Finally, I had it.

I was done being told that I was wrong, tired of being treated like I was an abnormality that needed fixing. I wanted to stop giving Nathan the power to tell me how I should feel.

But disentangling our decades-long marriage was terrifying. I'd never lived on my own before and, as the sole breadwinner, I didn't just want to kick Nathan to the curb, left to fend for himself. So, for four years between sitting in the counselor's office and officially divorcing, I consciously lived with a judgmental, angry man even though we no longer wanted to be together.

I used that time to take responsibility for my own happiness. I wanted to see if I could be happy no matter what anyone around me was doing, feeling, saying, or experiencing—especially him.

And, surprisingly, it wasn't his anger I needed to deal with. It was mine.

For four years, I watched as Nathan walked through the kitchen in a huff, throwing open a window because he didn't like the smell of the Indian spices I used for cooking. Or, I felt when he rolled his eyes at me behind my back in front of the kids. Each time he did it, I noticed anger bubbling up inside me, anger that I'd been taught to suppress and pretend wasn't there.

Really, he acted like the passive-aggressive, judgmental asshole he always was. The same man I'd been so happy to marry. But now, as he threw his metaphorical punches my way, I took note of my body and my feelings. No matter what he did, I asked myself if it was possible to keep my heart open.

Sometimes it was, sometimes it wasn't.

But that's how you do your work, you watch how you respond to everything and use those feelings to dig in and heal yourself. That's how you change your life for the better, even when nothing and no one around you changes.

By taking responsibility for my feelings, I realized that the reason our relationship wasn't working was because I was in it. I wasn't willing to have my own back because I was "keeping the peace." I was people-pleasing my way through life, pretending I didn't have wants and needs (which guaranteed I'd eventually explode). And I couldn't be fully intimate with Nathan without first knowing myself, no matter how much I pretended otherwise.

After our divorce, Nathan talked with each of our children individually about how angry I could be. He was right. When I finally saw the Truth, I realized his anger had nothing on mine.

But that made perfect sense because my dad was the only one in our household growing up who was allowed to do anger. When we got married, Nathan took on the role my dad played, while I was the perpetual Catholic good girl. I bottled up my anger until it had nowhere to go. I'd explode because the living room I'd just cleaned looked like a hotel room after a bachelorette party. Then I'd apologize for my existence and go back to desperately trying to be everything for everyone.

I'd never learned how to consciously be angry. I had no idea that when you brought awareness to anger, you didn't have to be as destructive as a tsunami. I didn't know how to deal with my feelings and have a voice for myself. I didn't know that having my own back meant I'd teach people how to treat me better (without unconsciously exploding at them).

And, until I lived with Nathan those last four years knowing we were going to get divorced, I didn't know how to take personal responsibility for my own happiness.

Happiness is a choice

When Nathan and I got married we thought, "Here's someone who really cares, chooses me, and creates a safe place for me to be me." We both hoped that marriage was going to make our lives easier and that we'd feel more secure.

And it did, we did—for a while.

We helped each other in all sorts of ways, offering advice, running a household together, and nurturing and comforting each other. We gave a lot.

But we were two kids in a trench coat playing at being a fully grown adult. It was codependency at its finest. He expressed the anger I couldn't touch while I played out the joy, happiness, and sadness he didn't have access to.

We were both innocent and completely clueless as to what we were doing and why.

Nathan was terrified of losing himself in our relationship, just like he had in his family of origin. So he plunged himself into his artwork as a socially acceptable way of distancing himself from me, which is precisely what terrified me the most—being abandoned and rejected.

The more he triggered in me, the more desperate and needy I became. And the more needy I became, the more reasons he found to lock himself in his studio, pushing everyone else away.

In the thick of it, it was impossible to explain our feelings or see beyond our filters of pain, let alone understand how the other person felt. I was too busy trying to convince him I was lovable, while he was too busy running away from his own messed up definition of love. And neither one of us knew we were doing it.

We were living a lie and the house of cards had to fall.

Because not knowing or expressing your feelings causes imbalance—those bottled up feelings have to go somewhere. Ignoring your emotions means ignoring what's coming up for you to heal. And, eventually, that shit gets so loud you can't ignore it anymore.

At the time, it was terrifying to acknowledge.

I could no longer ignore our codependency or how miserable we both were. But seeing everything I was playing out meant facing my terror of being abandoned and rejected by Nathan.

For a while, I desperately tried to get him to do his work to heal so I didn't have to face my core issues. Innocently, I wanted him to grow "along with me" so he wouldn't leave me as I changed.

But even when I shared energy sessions with Nathan that calmed and reset his nervous system, he had no skin in the game.

He was grateful for the support, but he didn't want to change. He didn't want to face his past. He thought having an angry edge kept him safe because when he'd let down his walls as a child he'd been shut down. Those scars still lingered.

Doing your work requires you to look at your past, to face the things that you don't want to admit were real, and to spend time processing those experiences in a safe space. It's uncomfortable and not everyone wants to do it.

But when you don't do your work, you'll spend your life reacting to triggers and getting your ass kicked. You'll waste time treating symptoms or trying to change the world rather than dealing with the core. That's a super painful way to live.

The reality is, you can't do someone else's work for them. You can only do your own.

I had no idea I was trying to get Nathan to change so I didn't have to, which just delayed my healing. I needed to face my own anger, my fear of abandonment and rejection, and the reality that not everyone wants to heal.

Living with Nathan for those four years, knowing we were going to get divorced, was a major part of doing my work.

I put Eckhart Tolle's quote, *"Relationships do not cause pain and unhappiness, they bring out the pain and unhappiness that is already in you,"* into action. I used that time to stop blaming Nathan for my unhappiness. And even though I messed up (often), I challenged myself to take responsibility for all my feelings. Eventually, I stopped giving myself a flimsy hall pass to be the victim, no matter how many times I fell back into it.

What I learned during those four years was that I couldn't sustainably be happy while suppressing my emotions. I needed to be honest with myself, remove my blinders, and stop plastering on a fake smile like my feelings didn't matter.

To make a change, I needed to build my muscles, grow my

awareness, and learn to meet and process all my feelings—including anger. The freeze responses I'd go into around anger as a child needed to be met and unpacked. I had to find new, empowered ways to show up open-heartedly and stop falling into my knee-jerk patterns.

I began to see all the ways I was deceiving myself—all the ways the terror of being abandoned and rejected controlled me. I let go of the happily-ever-after dream I wasn't really living.

As I did my work to unpack all the ways I was deceiving myself, I saw how emotionally unavailable I was—to myself. I saw how I didn't choose myself, how I abandoned and rejected myself all over the place, and how I thought it was my job to make Nathan happy so *then* I could be happy.

Once I unpacked those misunderstandings, I could choose to be happy, even when he was being a disconnected asshole.

And the more I faced the absolute terror of being abandoned and rejected—and stopped abandoning and rejecting myself—the better and better my life got. Each layer I faced brought more space and freedom.

Knowing better doesn't always mean doing better

You can read all the books, go to therapy, meditate, and stop talking to your parents entirely and you'll still bump up against the pain of your unconscious patterns.

You'll unknowingly re-create unresolved childhood issues at home, at work, with your spouse, with your own kids, or in the next book club you're invited to join. The ego will rear its ugly head and all the drama will puke itself out.

Why?

Because your ego, insulated pathways, limbic system, nervous system, and vagus nerve are all used to following the impulses of your patterns. Those patterns will play out again and again in your subconscious and unconscious mind until something interrupts them.

Only when you bring awareness to what you're doing and why, can you take conscious steps to create a new experience.

That means, even though you know you *should* drink the recommended amounts of water daily, you still don't stay hydrated because you're used to feeling groggy and sore, you're unconsciously running yourself ragged, or you don't want to deal with the inconvenience of having to pee more often.

It means that, even though you know you don't have the capacity to take on another job, you'll ask for more work because you've convinced yourself you need the money and you're so used to cycles of burnout you don't even know who you are without them.

It means that, even though you know you shouldn't get back together with your ex-boyfriend who stole your credit cards or cheated on you multiple times, you'll still be drawn to him because he helps you play out the patterns from your childhood you're used to.

Even if you "know" you're safe, if your nervous and limbic systems are in a state of fear, your body will fall into trauma responses like you've gone over a snow-filled hill on a butter-greased metal sled.

Until you process past experiences, release the charged emotions that are held in your body, and let go of BS lies, you'll stay stuck in childhood beliefs and conclusions that aren't even true. And until you face every layer, you'll bump up against triggers over and over and over again.

That's why, even as I was able to stand up to my father, I still had to face the same fear of abandonment and rejection with Nathan. I *knew* I didn't have to put up with his cruelty and insistence that I was wrong at every turn. But knowing something and doing it are two entirely different things. And it's really hard, until it's not.

When Nathan and I were married, I was the one who planned all the holidays, vacations, and family gatherings. After we divorced, I still invited Nathan over for the holidays. He had a hard time communicating with our children, and I still felt responsible for his relationship with them.

Then one Christmas, our son Thomas flew home from Florida.

At the time, Nathan was sharing an apartment with our eldest son, Matthew, so they could both afford a place to live. Matthew worked at a gym and had access to go work out on Christmas day. He invited his dad, his brother, and his sister to join him.

Thomas didn't have a car here, but while making plans, Nathan told Thomas and Julia to get their own ride. It was out of his way to come get them.

He lived three miles away.

Even though Thomas had flown more than a thousand miles to come home, Nathan was playing out the same shit he always did, acting like a victim and refusing to be inconvenienced because he had "healthy boundaries."

As someone who'd do most anything to share time and Love with our kids, I was blown away.

I'd carried the burden of Nathan's relationship with the kids for so long and finally saw just how little he showed up. Right then I decided to stop trying to make things easy for him and let him create his own experience with the children. I was done making excuses and hiding who he really was. I'd had enough.

It was a huge relief. But it also meant I had to change. It required me to let go of trying to protect the children from being disappointed by their dad.

Nathan didn't like it one bit.

In fact, his relationship with Thomas got so rocky that Nathan told me that he wasn't coming to our Thanksgiving dinner the next year because of it. I told him, "That works out well because you're not invited." I let him know I was done carrying his relationship with the kids.

But finding a new way was challenging.

I struggled at the thought of not making space for Nathan, of not inviting him to the holidays, or making it easy for him to see the children. I'd covered for his inability to develop and nurture healthy relationships with his kids for *decades*.

Dropping that responsibility meant I needed to change how I saw myself.

I had to let go of my old bullshit belief of what it meant to be a "good girl" and, once again, take responsibility for my own happiness. I had to disentangle yet another layer of our codependency.

After all the work I'd done, I *knew* I no longer had to give my power away to Nathan. But knowing better doesn't always mean doing better.

So it took me a while to start living it.

I have no regrets

Back in 2012, I ran into Nathan at the grocery store and updated him on what was going on with our children. Since he didn't communicate with them on his own, he was grateful to hear the tidbits.

In a moment of inspiration, I looked at him and said, "I'm so glad you're here and I can tell you this in person. As shitty as you treated me as a woman when we were married, I didn't think I deserved to be treated any better. That's on me."

I didn't say it to be cruel or mean to him. At all. I said it to take personal responsibility for my part in the whole dance. To let him know that I don't blame him—*how could I when I'm the one who taught him how to treat me based on what I thought I deserved?*

He obviously didn't see it that way. His lips got thin, his deep, DJ voice pitched high, and he completely shut down right before my eyes.

I never meant to hurt him. I wish him the best and I'm grateful for all we shared. The contrast was a gift to teach me what I did and didn't deserve, to help me do my work and heal.

In marrying him, I got to be with an angry man, just like my dad. I got to walk on eggshells with him, just like my mom walked on eggshells with my dad. He got to be righteous and a victim, just like his parents were righteous victims. (If they weren't happy, it was always someone or something else's fault.)

Because of Amy

I got to give my power away to Nathan and he got to pretend he was always "right" and justified in being angry. I got to shove down my anger and disappointment and blow my cork at the tiniest of things and he got to shut down when I exploded. Just like we'd been taught.

But I don't regret any of it.

I take 100 percent responsibility for being attracted to him, for playing out our matching patterns, and for not knowing any better... until I did.

Chapter 14
You Are Love

A decade into our marriage, I told Nathan I wanted diamond earrings. He told me I'd have to save up for them, so I did. A couple of years later, I finally had the money to buy myself a stunning pair of half-carat diamond earrings.

The next time we went to visit his parents, Nathan's mother chided me for not buying cubic zirconia instead, claiming, "No one else would know they aren't real."

I looked her straight in the eye and said, "I would."

For years, I'd put up with Nathan buying himself whatever he wanted. I turned a blind eye to how little I prioritized or spent on myself. And I never once questioned why that was.

Now, I wanted to drop the shame and live as if my wants and needs mattered. Through my mother-in-law's judgment, I could see how good it felt to choose and value myself—no matter what anyone else thought about it.

To this day, those earrings symbolize me choosing and Loving myself.

And I deserve that.

My life changed when I got radically honest with myself

Learning to find value in yourself, independent of what others say or think, is the core work of your life. It's freedom.

Wanting someone else to love, value, and respect you while you (often unknowingly) aren't Loving, valuing, and respecting yourself, simply won't work. Thinking you don't have any value unless someone else sees and validates you is painful and reckless.

Why?

Because you can't control how anyone else feels about you.

And even if they do Love, value, and respect you, you won't believe them if you don't already feel that way about yourself. You'll just assume they're telling you what you want to hear so they can get what they want. Or, you'll think that they do mean it, but they must not know the *real* you.

In other words, someone else's Love can't heal your core wounds. Even when they freely give it, the elevated feeling of goodness won't last. That's why they call it the honeymoon phase.

Believing someone else determines your value is giving away the keys to your castle.

The Truth is, you're Lovable whether or not you know it, feel it, believe it, live it, taste it, or touch it. You're valuable whether anyone else knows it—or not. Love is the fabric of your existence.

Reflecting on my younger self, I see how I chased and begged Nathan to love and value me. As a child, I did the same with my father, vying for his approval. It's what I was taught to do. At the time, it was impossible for me to grasp that their anger and unhappiness had nothing to do with me. I didn't understand that I desperately wanted them to love and value me, even though I didn't Love and value myself.

In order to make the changes I said I wanted, I had to get radically honest with myself about what I was playing out—and why.

That meant I had to fully name and face all my feelings to clear the blocks to Love. Even if I didn't tell anyone else I was hurting, I had to at least acknowledge it for myself.

But the more I accepted my feelings, the less shame I felt about having them. The less I ran from my emotions, the more I could use them as information about what was coming up for me to heal—and the easier I could let go of the pain and struggle and return to Love.

I could've sped up the process of self-Love a zillion times faster had I known and worked through this core Truth: "I am valuable, whether someone else values me or not."

So are you.

In the words of Matt Kahn, "You deserve more Love, not less."

You are Love. You are Loved. And thinking you're any less than the magnificent creature you are is living a lie.

There is no magic button

People often turn to sugar, food, alcohol, drugs, work, sex, etc. because, without that disconnect, they're unable to cope with life and the messy feelings coming up.

But, no matter what the songs say, there's no such thing as comfortably numb.

Either you're open to being present and experiencing life, or you're shut down, disconnected, and unable to take in the joy because you're too busy running from the pain.

Yes, it's uncomfortable or even terrifying to start to feel your feelings—especially when you've been taught to avoid them your entire life. But consider the alternative.

Feeling allows you to live instead of pretending you're living as you wait to die.

The good news is, your feelings aren't the Truth of who you are, they're just showing you what's coming up for you to heal. You don't have to make them wrong. You don't have to let them consume you or send you into the shitter.

Feeling your feelings isn't about wallowing in your room for a decade because your husband cheated on you. It's not about reck-lessly spewing every feeling you've ever had at the next family reunion. And it's not about rehashing your dad's death from when you were six years old over and over, falling farther into a spiral of depression every time.

It's about finding a safe place to acknowledge your feelings and bring compassion and understanding to them because that's how you'll heal.

As you give yourself permission to feel your feelings, you'll start processing them.

Magically, that's when you'll stop blaming everyone else for your pain, waiting around for them to change, or getting drunk to numb yourself so you can hang out with your family. You'll feel more "plugged in" and connected to the spark of life around you, inspired to create, and joyful to be alive. You'll look back at the time your mom kicked you out of the house for disobeying her and it won't induce a panic attack like it always used to.

Through feeling, you actually inhabit your body. You're present. Free.

This connection is what you've always wanted and what you've hungered for. It's what you thought would come from the new job, getting a divorce, leaving the country, or cutting your bangs. And best of all, it's real. Because it's you.

But finding your way back to yourself takes time.

How can you have confidence in something you've never done before? How can you trust yourself when you've been taught to deny your own wants and needs? Who are you when you've spent so much time avoiding your feelings that you recklessly thought the next rela-tionship, vacation, or home renovation would fill the void? How do you come back online when you've spent your whole life thinking winning best-in-show with your labradoodle would be the thing that finally made you happy—and it didn't?

You don't start body-building with 500-pound weights, you start with the bar.

When you've spent your entire life lacking confidence and self-trust, you can't just hit some magic button and start trusting yourself, feeling connected, and having a zest for life.

Trust and confidence are earned. They come on the other side of having done the things you're terrified of. They're built up over time as you learn to connect with and listen to yourself. When you've spent your whole life giving your power away to everyone and their brother's gerbil, it's going to take time. It's even healthy not to trust yourself or have confidence while you stumble through.

Doing your work is a practice.

And when you start, every step improves your life in ways you can't even begin to imagine right now.

You are Love

If your childhood was anything like mine, you've been taught that love means giving until it hurts and giving some more.

You've been taught that love comes from outside yourself. And, like all the romance novels and movies imply, if you're not in a relationship, you won't experience love, and you're going to die alone and miserable.

You've been taught that love is ignoring your own wants and needs because if you act *that* way it "gives mommy a headache," or "makes daddy mad." With that misunderstanding, you think love means losing yourself and pretending to be someone who never has feelings and certainly doesn't cry.

You've been taught that you're responsible for other people's thoughts, feelings, actions, and inactions. So, love is making sure other people feel loved because *they* deserve it—but you don't because you haven't done enough to earn it (yet).

But none of that's real.

Like the book *A Course in Miracles* says, when you boil it down, only two things exist—Love and fear, and only one of them is real.

Love is who you are, it's who everyone is. It's what you're made of down to your DNA. Love is the core of your being, your spiritual essence, the spark of your Soul.

Call it what you want—God, Qi, Prana, Energy, Universal Intelligence, Creation—it's all the same thing, and it all boils down to Love.

Love is remembering your magnificence (without comparing yourself to others so you can be the victim of the bullshit story that *they* have it all figured out and you're way behind).

And, if Love is who you are, fear is everything keeping you from remembering it.

Fear is the guilt, the shame, the memories from when your family insisted you were hard to love. It's the misunderstanding that you have to work harder than everyone else to "earn" love. It's the bullshit belief that love comes from others instead of deep within.

But when you release the held trauma, bullshit stories, pain, and lies (in other words, the fear), all that remains is your connection to God, Qi, Prana, Universal Intelligence. All that remains is Love.

When you know you're responsible for Loving yourself, you don't need anyone else to bolster your sense of self-worth or make you feel safe. They get to be themselves—and you don't have to feel hurt or inadequate because of something they say, do, or don't do. You'll stop caring about what they think about you, and when you do, you become freer and more confident. Regardless of how they act, you'll be easier to get along with too, since you'll no longer feel the need to be a defensive asshole.

When you Love yourself, you're open to receiving more Love, exactly as people are able to give it. You'll no longer take it personally when your dad acknowledges your birthday with a generic card signed only "dad." You'll either accept how emotionally unavailable he is and appreciate that he even got you a card, or use it as an opportunity to ask for what you want—a birthday card that includes all the mush and gush—without being tied to whether he gives it to you or not.

When you Love yourself, you'll share Love with others more

readily, even if it means Loving them from a distance so you can avoid the drama, pain, and BS lies they're unknowingly playing out.

Loving myself made all the difference

In 2013, a year after my divorce from Nathan, I flew to Turks & Caicos.

At the time, I knew I needed to go, but I had no idea why. It wasn't about being a tourist—at all. It was about unplugging from my day-to-day, tucking into a warm space with sandy beaches and rolling ocean waves, and just being.

But the minute I sat on the plane, I started bawling. For all the work I'd done, my feelings once again blindsided me. It hit me that, in order to make space for what came next, I needed to say goodbye to my life and everything in it. It was like facing my own death.

Actually, I was okay with dying. This was worse.

The terror of ceasing to exist consumed me as I said goodbye to my children, my home, my pets, my business, my bank account, and everything I knew my life to be.

It didn't mean that my children would never talk to me again or that I'd lose everything. But I had to release the fear, burden, and bullshit stories I carried about those things. The fear of not having enough money, the story that I needed to remodel my kitchen before my home was what it "should" be, the belief that I was a "bad" mom if I didn't "fix" my children's problems when they were in pain...I had to let go of it all.

Much like processing Amy's death in the hotel room years before, I had to make space to feel all my feelings and see my life in a brand new way. And it knocked me on my ass.

For five days, I couldn't even leave my Airbnb. I acknowledged all the ways I tried to make Nathan happy—and how that was never going to work. I saw how recklessly I'd given away my power hoping he'd make me happy. And I realized I could never be someone else's source or make them mine.

I took personal responsibility for not believing I deserved any better.

I embraced these feelings from my past, brought them into the light of consciousness, and stopped avoiding the feelings that had haunted me my whole life.

I stopped looking for anyone else to be my answer or to give me the intimacy and connection I craved.

I chose to Love myself.

It was such deep inner work, I couldn't even leave to get food until the sixth day. I holed up in this private bungalow, mostly naked, barely doing anything more than feeling my feelings, living off the crackers, trail mix, uncooked rice, baked potatoes, and teabags I'd brought with me.

To really let go of the limitations, the filters, the BS beliefs I'd been carrying for so long, I needed to feel the emotional abuse (from Nathan and all the ways I abused myself), to welcome it with an open, tender heart, to safely share my story—with myself—and be transformed in the presence of Love.

In the past, I ignored my inner knowing and I called it love. It wasn't Love. I just didn't want to face inconvenient Truths. I couldn't or didn't want to see all the ways I wasn't Loving myself. I didn't want to see how I was exactly like my dad, being handed Love and pushing it away because I didn't think I deserved it.

By the end of my trip, I finally believed, in the core of my being, that I was simply *enough*. I didn't have to do anything to be worthy. I just am.

And, in Loving and seeing myself, my former marriage, and my life in Truth, I paved the way for a new, truly intimate relationship with myself.

Even then I could see the impact Loving myself would have on any future relationship I chose to be in, all because I related to myself in such a new, Loving way.

Here's an entry from my journal in Turks & Caicos:

I married myself.

It was a whim. It took all of three seconds to have the thought and act on it intentionally.

I am married.

That means I get to Love me and cherish me until death do us part. But really, even death won't separate me from me. I will just leave this beautiful shell of a body that I deeply Love and appreciate.

Now, in the meantime, if there are other available Souls to adventure within this thing called life, I will consider walking this path with them.

Because I Love me so much, the Souls I freely give of my time and myself need to have large capacities of Love to share with themselves and with me.

I have spent so much time looking for others to disappoint me.

Now my internal compass is being reoriented to allow others to share their Love with me...

And to actually take it in...

And from that place of fullness continue to share my infinite Love with them. Hmmm.

What a juicy Love affair.

So satisfying too.

The idea that Love comes from outside of you is a limitation.

Movies, love songs, romance novels teach us that love must come from someone else, that we aren't whole without *their* love.

But Love isn't about losing yourself. It doesn't require you to give until it hurts and give some more. You're just as deserving of Love as everyone else.

When you can't see Love, when you aren't experiencing it, touching it, feeling it for yourself, it's just a misunderstanding.

Love is without limitation. It's infinite. It's all there is.

Learning to Love yourself is the ultimate journey of intimacy

Divorcing after twenty-seven years of marriage wasn't a loss. I don't regret it. Because being in a relationship where there wasn't room for me to be me showed me all the ways I wasn't open to a Loving, intimate connection.

From that experience, I gained a deep respect, understanding, and Love for myself. What could be better? Through surrendering my bullshit patterns, stories, and beliefs of what I thought my life should look like, I reclaimed myself.

The irony isn't lost on me. Loss of self *was* my motivator to reclaim myself.

And, it was worth it.

All the contrast, pain, ignorance, denial, avoiding, and pretending led me to Truth. It gave me the courage and grace to move forward. It taught me how to have a Loving, intimate connection—with myself.

Mine was simply a journey. On the journey I was asleep. I fought to wake up and did—in moments. Eventually, I anchored into more and more moments of wakefulness. They were delightful. They inspired me to keep going.

And, while this journey will take you to uncomfortable places and require you to face thoughts, beliefs, and feelings about yourself that were never true, it's also a journey filled with satisfaction and joy. It offers a lifetime of rewards.

That's what doing your work is all about, connecting with yourself.

It's seeing what you're doing and why, and healing the parts of you keeping you from the juicy, intimate Love affair you crave—with yourself. Only then can you cultivate Loving, intimate relationships with others.

Chapter 15
You Are Loved

The day before my divorce from Nathan was finalized, a dear friend of mine from New Jersey called me up out of the blue.

We hadn't spoken in eight years, but Karl and I went way back. In the past, I'd opened up to him about how Amy's death helped me treasure every moment. And when he called me, he said he was so deeply grateful for his own life, his job, the PRs he'd hit at the gym, and a kitchen remodel that gave him the kitchen of his dreams, that he had to share.

He said he knew I was the only person who could understand the depth of gratitude he felt.

A year later, we were still in touch, and he asked me what I wanted. Without thought, "I want you to come live with me," flew out of my mouth. It felt like a scene from a movie where a character slaps their hands over their mouth after hearing their own honesty. I couldn't believe what I said, but I knew it was true.

A few months later—sixteen years since I'd last seen him in person—Karl packed up his life, drove across the country, and pulled into my driveway.

We've been together ever since.

It shouldn't have worked...but it did

When I first asked Karl to move in, my daughter Julia still lived with me. She was fiercely protective of me, so much so that she'd throw herself between me and any man who even looked my way.

From the salesman at the Toyota dealership to the guy in Homemakers helping me measure a couch, no one was good enough for me in her eyes (not that I was interested in any of them either, but that didn't stop her from getting pissed at them for hitting on me).

So even though I wanted Karl to move in, if Julia wasn't ok with it, it wasn't happening. She needed to feel comfortable in her own home.

When I asked her what she thought, she said, "Yeah, feels great."

I was stunned. She'd met Karl back when she was four years old and, at the time, told me, "Karl Loves me," but her go-to reaction to men interested in me was to physically get between us. And here she was whole-heartedly agreeing to let him move in. She knew as well as I did that it was meant to be.

On the other hand, one of my mentors told me that relationships where you don't really know the other person are short-lived. He said it would never work.

And, frankly, it shouldn't have.

Who uproots their entire life to be with someone they haven't seen in sixteen years? Who asks someone they've never lived with to move across the country and expects a happy ending? I'd never recommend it to anyone.

But there's a difference between our story and all the movies coming out of Hollywood.

I can say, without a doubt, that my relationship with Karl only works because of the intense amount of internal work I did to have an intimate relationship with myself. Well that, and Karl's willingness to change and grow, and our deep desire to be with each other.

We wouldn't be together without it.

For me, getting through the growing pains, bumps, anger, and misunderstandings that come from being in an intimate relationship was possible because I processed my core issues of abandonment and rejection and continued to do my work with Karl as I was triggered. I wasn't hell-bent on changing him. I didn't need to make him wrong for who he was. And I knew he couldn't be my answer.

A lot of women I know find a man and pretend he's who they want him to be. Hell, it's what I did in my first marriage for more than two decades. But, after seeing how spectacularly that failed, I wasn't going to repeat the same thing with Karl.

I don't need my partner to be enlightened. I need someone who shows up as real, wants to be with me, and cares about his heart as well as mine. That's Karl.

I Love him for who he is *because* I Love myself so deeply.

One time Julia asked him, "What's it like being with my mom?"

Karl shot back, "A lot of men think they want to be with your mom. They're idiots. In order to be with her, you have to know who you are."

What can I say? You can't be intimate with someone else until you're intimate with yourself.

I Love Loving Karl—and we're very different people

Karl and I first met way back in 1996.

I was thirty years old, working as a project manager at an insurance company, and he was the conversion manager working for the vendor we'd chosen for our new computer system. Since he lived all the way on the East Coast, we spent months on the phone discussing details, system requirements, and the flow of migrating data before meeting in person.

I found out later that, because of my deeper voice, he thought I was a fifty-year-old woman with stockings that bunched at my swollen ankles (boy, was he surprised).

When we finally met in person, Karl was sitting in our makeshift "war room" that the vendors tucked into. He stood up, took a bow, and said, "Ma'am, it's a pleasure to meet you."

And that's Karl for you.

He's the most intelligent person I've ever met. At eight years old, he read the *World Book Encyclopedias* and still remembers most of it. At fifteen, he read *The Lord of The Rings: The Return of the King*, and to this day he can recite aloud the Battle of the Pelanor Fields by memory.

Once Karl's been somewhere, he won't need a map to navigate—even years later. And though he'll claim his memory isn't as good as it used to be, he can more or less recall any recipe he's made once, right down to the correct number of teaspoons.

Basically, he'll kick your ass in bar trivia.

Meanwhile, I'm an intuitive guide and energy healer who's all about feelings. I read energies, and because I've done so much work clearing my own traumas, triggers, and BS stories, I support others who are stuck in pain by clearing the shit from their past they're too afraid to face on their own.

I could walk into a room and tell you what's going on with every single person in it (and actually, I don't even have to be in the room). My BS meter is off the charts—even when you're lying to yourself.

Basically, I'm a human lie detector.

Karl and I are stronger together, but the first two years after he hit the door to my house were hard, to say the least.

We Love each other and wanted to be together, but we had to figure out how to communicate. And for Karl, that was rough.

Innocently, he thought we couldn't talk before bed because he needed a good night's sleep before work the next day. We couldn't talk in the morning because he had to work. And we couldn't talk on the weekends because the mailman was coming at noon.

I was like, "Ok, when can we talk?"

Because if I was going to be with someone, I wanted to relate to them. I wanted to understand them and know what they were thinking and how they felt, and to be understood in turn whether we agreed or not. I wanted intimacy beyond just moving through the day, feeling butt-hurt because I didn't understand his motivations. I tried that for twenty-seven years and it sucked.

But for two years, whenever I told Karl how I felt, he thought I was telling him it was his fault.

One night on a walk around the neighborhood, I laid it out for him. If we wanted to make this work, we had to get comfortable with the "hard" conversations—regardless of whether or not the mailman was on his way. Because I'd done so much work to heal myself, I (mostly) didn't make him wrong. I (mostly) wasn't taking his actions personally. I just wanted a deeper connection.

Later that evening, Karl's deep brown eyes, with just a hint of green, stared into mine as he said, "I know that in order to be with you I'll have to grow. So, I'll grow."

My whole body sighed in relief.

Finally, after being with someone who couldn't choose me, love me, or meet me, I was with someone who not only wanted to be with me, but who knew being with me meant getting comfortable being uncomfortable, who knew he had to change and grow, and who wanted to.

Living in reality, not a fantasy

Karl used to get pissed at me for not loading the dishwasher "correctly" or for taking my time in the grocery store. He still hates the way I bag our groceries. And when we travel, he can redline faster than it would take a driver in New York City to honk at you when the light turns green.

Though he's going gray now, Karl will always be my fiery redhead. And I Love him for it.

But, I also know I don't deserve to take the brunt of his anger just because I Love him and I'm a safe space.

One time, on a cruise, he was waiting on me to grab a bite to eat. I went to let my daughter Julia know what we were doing, and before I could slip away, she introduced me to another couple who were joining us for dinner. I kept the social graces short, but it was longer than Karl wanted.

When I got back to him, he was pissed and started to take it out on me.

I looked at him and said, "I'm a grown-ass woman. You're not my father, and I don't deserve to be treated like a child. If you wanted to leave and go eat, you could've. And if you were in my position, you would've done the same thing."

Thankfully, even though he isn't really interested in doing his work in the same way I do, he's self-aware enough that he heard me and made a change. Otherwise, we wouldn't be together.

It's not about making Karl wrong or vilifying him. (He teaches me how to treat him too.) It's about knowing who we are, Loving ourselves first, and bringing that Love into our relationship. It's about being willing to be wrong, to grow, to change. It's about knowing deep in our core that we want what's best for the other person and that we'd never do anything to consciously hurt each other's hearts. And it's about seeing our relationship for what it is—not for some Hollywood fantasy.

You may not want what I want. That's ok. I'm not handing you a blueprint for the "perfect relationship." You get to decide what a Loving partnership looks like for you.

But building a life with someone can be challenging, whether you've known and loved them for more than thirty years or you just met yesterday.

Why? Because *everyone's* operating from their own filters. We all have a particular way of looking at the world. We all have built-in beliefs, misunderstandings, BS lies, stories, and misperceptions we don't even know are there, that don't have *anything* to do with whoever we're with.

To really be with someone, you have to unravel all that—or at the very least be willing to work through it. Otherwise, you'll constantly trigger the shit out of each other and not know why. You'll run from relationship to relationship (or job to job, vacation to vacation, book club to book club) and never feel satisfied. Or, you'll think you're happy, but really just coexist with your partner. You'll use the other person to feed those filters and spend your life trying to convince yourself your shitty marriage is a happily-ever-after dream come true.

Yes, it can be super uncomfortable looking at and unpacking your own beliefs, BS lies, and filters. It can put a strain on your relationship when you start to change and they don't want you to. And, if you're not with someone who's open to Truth or willing to grow, and you can't accept and Love them exactly as they are, it can tear you apart.

You'll only be willing to stand your ground when you first believe in your core that you're worth it, that you deserve to be Loved, and that, if someone can't Love you exactly as you are, maybe they're not right for you.

Remember, you can use your relationships to heal and grow or to lose yourself. The choice is yours.

You are Loved

Before Karl moved across the country, a client mentioned how shocked he was that I wasn't with someone. He said, "You have so much Love to give. Why aren't you with someone?"

I looked at him and simply replied, "I haven't been open to it."

Until I did my work, I wasn't open to someone intimately and emotionally available.

For years, I *thought* I wanted to be with someone who loved me. That I wanted to be cherished, worshiped, and accepted by a man. Instead, I chose someone angry, hurtful, mean, self-absorbed, and mistrustful.

Someone who reflected back to me my childhood and what I thought I deserved.

Nathan couldn't fully love me because he didn't fully Love himself. But I didn't know I was attracted to him because I constantly had to convince him I was lovable. I wouldn't have chosen someone emotionally available who could see and appreciate me because I wasn't emotionally available to myself.

I didn't know I wanted to feel abandoned and rejected, to be with someone angry and inconsiderate of how I might feel, to be made wrong, and to feel like I wasn't enough no matter how much I did.

That's what I was used to. That's what I thought love was.

When I finally saw the Truth of what I was playing out and why, I stopped letting my BS beliefs, filters, and stories run the show.

That's when I finally let myself see how Lovable I truly am.

Healing myself opened me up to a healthy, balanced, intimate relationship. One where I'm cherished and worshiped by an open-hearted man who can truly see me, accept me, respect me, and Love me with all of his heart—because he Loves himself (except when he can't, and then I call him on it).

Loving relationships with others are a reflection of a healthy, balanced, intimate relationship with yourself. And when you don't Love yourself, your relationships will reflect that back to you. You'll look for the unavailable and blame them for your unhappiness.

You deserve to be seen, known, Loved, and understood. And you're the only one who can truly give that to yourself. Anyone else Loving you is just a bonus after you've done your work.

Love starts with you

Unless you want to live alone on a mountaintop or never leave your house, you're going to be in relationships. And relationships bring out the triggers that are already inside you (often in increasingly annoying ways until you finally pay attention).

But here's a secret: Everyone Loves you, whether they know it or not. When it seems like they don't, or they lash out, it's the pain inside them begging for more Love.

What matters more is how *you* feel about their words, actions, or inactions. Because you can use the triggers they bring out in you to blame the other person and wait until they change so *then* you can be happy. Or, you can use the triggers to lean in and do your work to heal.

Only one of those choices leads you to the life you've always wanted.

Chapter 16
If I Can Do This Work, Anyone Can

For the most part, I've always been a happy person.

Despite everything, it's not like my entire life was filled with pain and misery. But even during the "good" times, an overshadowing cloud of abandonment and rejection seeped into all my relationships and kept me from being me. It kept me from the love I desperately wanted.

I spent so much time and energy arguing for the view of the world I'd grown up seeing. The one where I'd been taught that men were more important than women, that I had to work harder than everyone else to "earn" their love, that I wasn't worthy of it anyway.

As Richard Bach said, "Argue for your limitations and, sure enough, they're yours."

But I didn't even know I was doing it.

I didn't know I walked on eggshells around men so they wouldn't get angry. I didn't know I tried to manipulate others into loving me so I wouldn't be abandoned and rejected. I didn't know I abandoned and rejected myself all over the place. I didn't know I thought it was my job to make everyone else happy before I could be happy.

Then Amy died and everything I thought about life was turned upside down. I was changed forever.

Because of Amy

People think pain is wrong because it's uncomfortable, but that's a huge misunderstanding. Making pain wrong will kick your ass over and over and over again.

Pain isn't wrong. It's a part of life.

And, even when pain does show up, it's not the end of the story. You're still writing it. You don't have to stay stuck in pain.

Losing Amy was the hardest thing I've ever experienced. And it was an absolute gift. She broke my heart all the way open so I could finally find a new way.

Because of Amy, I could no longer sit in my limitations. I could no longer identify with the lies I told myself, play small, or be the disempowered victim.

Sure, it took me eleven years of really digging into my core issues, but life on the other side was a bazillion times better—because it was *mine*.

Years after she died, one of my mentors, Jonathan Parker, told me that Amy's consciousness was that of an Ascended Master. He reads energies and told me that Amy wanted to escort Julia onto this planet because they'd been together many lifetimes. But, as Jonathan said, "Amy was never meant to stay."

As soon as I heard it, I knew it was true.

The pain of losing Amy was my greatest teacher. And, as painful as it was, I'm beyond grateful for the gift—for being Amy's mother, for being shown what it means to show the fuck up and really live.

Because of her life *and her death*, I found energy work. And through doing my work, I released the traumas, triggers, held emotions, and core issues keeping me from being present, open to, and grateful for all of life. I faced, shifted, and transformed my old patterns of feeling unlovable, and unworthy. I was able to meet and Love myself at such a deep and profound level I never had access to before.

How could I ever make that wrong?

It takes a decade—at least

You're the common factor in all your relationships, your job, and your experiences.

You could cheat on your partner, quit your job and get a new one, flee the country, or take up a side hustle guaranteed to make you millions and you'd still feel the same way you do now—even if it takes a while as you find exciting ways to distract yourself.

You're the problem. But that's actually good news. Why? Because that means you're also the solution.

And if you're the solution, your life doesn't have to be hard. You don't have to struggle. Your relationships, your job, your experiences can be easy *because you're in them*. All it takes is doing your work to face your feelings, heal your past, and release the traumas you don't know are kicking your ass.

But, when you first start doing your work, your ego will push back. It wants to keep you safe, but it has shit consciousness. It thinks keeping you safe means keeping you small, stuck, and in pain because that's what you know.

To your ego, a soggy cracker is better than no cracker.

That means, to have a new experience, you're going to have to unravel everything you think you know about yourself, everything you're innocently ignorant of, and all the patterns you don't even know are running the show. You're going to have to expand your awareness and look at what you're doing—and why—in Truth (not from your filters of pain and struggle).

It means reframing every time you're triggered.

Instead of blaming someone else (even when they're an asshole), take responsibility for your feelings. Instead of staying pissed at your boss for denying you a raise, ask yourself what you're afraid of. Instead of waiting for enough time to pass so you won't be sad that your mom died (which isn't how that works, by the way), find a healer who can help you feel and process the grief. Instead of asking everyone else to love you, look at all the ways you don't really Love yourself and lean into that.

It means being willing to face the death of every part of you that isn't Love.

This work takes a decade—or more—because letting go of the BS stories, lies, and misunderstandings you don't even know you're living with is really hard... until it's not.

Most people walk around thinking they have their answer. They know themselves. They're already happy. And the only thing they *really* need is to lose five pounds, go on vacation, get a haircut, quit their job, or find a Lover.

They don't know that none of that will make them happy—at least not sustainably.

What you're after in life, what we're all after, is connection. That connection first comes from a connection with yourself. But you'll never do that if you're too busy letting all your triggers run the show.

If you don't know you believe men are more important than women, you'll constantly give your power away to men and be bitter, angry, and resentful. If you don't know you think you have to work harder than everyone else to "earn" their love, you'll keep working hard waiting for someone else to see and love you. If you're afraid of being abandoned and rejected, you'll have to abandon and reject yourself all over the place to keep everyone else from leaving you.

Honestly looking at those things will be uncomfortable. Facing the pain often feels shitty.

But every time you release a held emotion, let go of a story you thought was true, kill an identity you thought made you *you*, or stop blaming someone else for your guilt, frustration, and rage and instead unpack those feelings for yourself, you'll improve your life. You'll expand into more freedom. You'll feel more Love, joy, peace, and connection with everyone in your life.

When you see the pattern again and again, you can either put your blinders on and pretend everyone else in your life is the problem and you're the victim. Or you can do your work, change your brain (your entire operating system), and finally have a new experience—whether anyone else changes or not.

On the other side, you'll feel deeply connected, grateful, and empowered with more space for happiness. You'll improve every relationship in your life, you'll stop waiting around for everyone else to change, or stop expecting them to be your answer. You'll accept them exactly as they are.

You won't get pulled into the drama of high highs and low lows. You'll follow inspiration, guidance, and be able to go with the flow no matter what's going on around you.

And you'll stop getting caught up in your thoughts—because if you keep doing your work, eventually, they'll go away entirely.

Doing my work gave me my life

Even when I knew the power of this work, trusted it, and experienced firsthand how my life changed from it, I still tripped all over myself.

I *knew* every relationship was a reflection of my relationship with myself, but I'd still find myself wanting everyone else (especially men) to see, love, value, respect, understand, and accept me when I wasn't doing any of those things for myself.

I still fell into patterns, hit new blocks, and got triggered in increasingly annoying ways.

But I kept digging in. For eleven years, even when I faltered, I took responsibility for my feelings, I meditated (*a lot*), I expanded my awareness, and I brought Love to myself over and over again.

Eventually, I "lost" my mind. The voice in my head went quiet. I stopped having thoughts—the mental chatter disappeared. I released enough triggers that I'm now present and not sucked into ego-drama all the time. I anchored into the emptiness, which is nothing and everything all at once.

It's like being in a constant state of meditation.

When I brush my teeth, I feel every bristle over my gums and the water swishing through my teeth. When I step outside, I'm one with every branch swaying in the wind, the sound of every lawn mower or leaf blower filling the air, and the smell of freshly cut grass.

The world around me is so vibrant and stunning and alive. It doesn't matter what I'm doing, I'm connected to and one with everything. There is no good or bad, no right or wrong, no drama.

I'm still human. I still get tired and my blood sugar gets low when I don't eat enough. I still get triggered (though it's rare). I still grieve the loss of people I Love. But I accept whatever life throws my way and surrender to all of it, even when it's painful or annoying, even when someone criticizes me, even when someone I Love is in pain. I'm still in the emptiness.

Most people have no idea they can live in this state all the time.

You likely already have moments when you're sitting by the ocean listening to the waves crash into the shore or looking up at the sky full of stars and feel connected to the whole of the Universe. You might hear a baby giggle or let a friend cry on your shoulder after a bad breakup and have your heart fly open in Love, compassion, and gratitude for life.

Those are the moments of enlightenment when your heart is blown open and you can't help but be in the here and now, remembering that you are Love.

And when you do your work, you expand those moments until they're all you experience.

That's when it won't matter what's going on around you, it's not the end of the story. You'll know, deep in your core, that this is your divine life. Whatever's coming up is just the next layer to be unpacked.

That's what I mean when I say this work gave me my life. I mean I live in the emptiness, that my ego doesn't control me, that I'm not tossed about by the drama. I live a guided and surrendered life where I only do what I'm inspired to do.

Even death doesn't control me anymore. Because I've faced not only Amy's death but my own so many times in so many ways that I'm free to release the fear and sink into Love.

If I can do this work, anyone can

My daughter Julia likes to say, "If my mom can do this work, anyone can."

She's right. I'm not uniquely qualified. I'm not special. I don't have some advantage you'll never have access to.

The only thing I had that most people don't, was the courage and willingness to face my past because the pain, restlessness, and disconnect were so intolerable. It was my hunger and dedication to see Truth, my refusal to stay stuck when I knew that accepting and processing the pain would lead to a freer, more joyful experience on the other side. It was my willingness to face the death of everything I thought I knew over and over and over again.

Really, I'm no different from you.

When my kids were growing up, one of the lines I often fed them was, "You may need counseling for this later, but I'm doing the best I can."

And I was.

But then I found energy work and I didn't have to get sucked into the traumas, triggers, BS stories, and misunderstandings that used to send me into a tailspin.

Over time, I no longer put up with being treated so poorly in my marriage, by my dad, or by myself. I stopped chasing my kids to see, value, and love me—I just Loved them anyway. I stopped walking through the world as if I had to cater to men and as if their opinions were more important than mine.

That's when my dad stopped trying to pull me into his controlling bullshit (or, when he did, I didn't care). It's when Nathan finally admitted he wanted a divorce. It's when I stopped being attracted to emotionally unavailable men and married Karl—even though I thought I'd never get married again.

And, yes, I fell on my ass a lot. I reverted back to my old patterns over and over. I considered Karl's pizza topping preferences before asking myself what I wanted (until I saw what I was doing and finally cut the crap).

But the more blocks I released, the better my life got.

In the emptiness, the triggers aren't dramatic, they can feel like shit, but they're just the next layer. They're showing me what I have to dig into and process so I can expand into even deeper levels of freedom I never knew existed before.

Doing my work *was* my therapy. Because living my life with Love and Truth enabled me to do the thing Amy handed me so plainly when I was crying in the tub all those years ago:

To show the fuck up and really live.

When I let go of everything I thought I knew about myself, my life, the world, and everyone in it, I made space for Love, gratitude, and presence. I was able to not only feel—but also live—the oneness of everything in the Universe. And I'm able to hold space for anyone on this planet to face and shift their deepest pain, fear, and trauma— because I courageously faced and shifted my own. You can have that too.

That's the power of doing your work.

I'm not qualified to judge you—I'm only qualified to Love

In Truth, no one can "make" you feel anything.

You might think you're only upset because so and so "made" you feel bad by not taking out the trash or not doing their fair share at work.

They're just showing you what's already inside you that's coming up to be healed. You wouldn't get triggered by them not taking out the trash if you weren't afraid that it meant they didn't love or respect you. You wouldn't get pissy about what other people did at work if it didn't trigger your past where your dad taught you you were only as worthy as the shit you got done. You'd have a voice for yourself, stand up for what you deserved, and respond as inspired—without the drama.

The reason I can take anyone through their deepest pain is because I've faced my core issues—abandonment and rejection, self-judgment, and self-hatred—so fully that I have no judgment or hatred to bring to you.

There's only Love.

When you do your work and take responsibility for your feelings, you'll be empowered to live your life—not a life controlled by those triggers.

And when you do, you'll open to Loving yourself fully, you'll finally realize that Love is who you are—even when you can't see, taste, touch, or experience it for yourself.

Once you do, you'll be able to Love everyone else for who they are—whether or not they change. You stop blaming other people and the world for your feelings, you won't feel the need to judge them either. You'll just Love and accept them—exactly as they are, even if you Love them from a distance.

Why? Because you Love yourself.

And So It Is...

When I first found energy work, I was home. I couldn't get enough. It was the Truth I'd always wanted. Nothing else in life ever made as much sense.

Energy work so clearly demonstrates Einstein's theory that everything is energy and energy isn't created or destroyed, it's simply transformed. It shows you the subtle and not-so-subtle energy patterns you're playing out so you don't have to keep living with them for another decade—or two (unless you want to).

Like how abandonment and rejection followed me in all my relationships until I finally acknowledged and processed all the ways I recklessly abandoned and rejected myself. When I stopped abandoning and rejecting myself, I didn't tolerate other people treating me like shit.

Doing your work is all about identifying the issues (awareness), dis-identifying from the lies, bringing compassion, understanding, and Love to the past versions of you who didn't know any better. It's about shifting your consciousness around the previously held beliefs, thoughts, and stories. It's about releasing the held emotions, trauma, and misunderstandings you don't even know you're hanging onto.

That's how you have a totally new experience with life: by

removing all the blocks to experiencing your goodness, opening up to the Love you already are, and expanding the times you feel enlightened.

It's taking personal responsibility for yourself because that *is* personal empowerment.

We all want connection. And connection comes from being connected and intimate with yourself, which comes from doing your work. That's why energy work is the most practical thing on the planet. But it's a process—and one that takes time to work through.

And in our humanity, very few people want to look at the Truth of their existence or take the time to do this work. Why? Two reasons:

1) You often don't even know that it's possible to live your life with a greater level of happiness and freedom (or you're convinced you're already happy even when you're not).

2) You're too afraid to let the house of cards you've spent a lifetime building fall. Once you see the Truth, there is no unseeing it. And you might not be ready for *everything* to change.

But if you keep showing up and doing the work to clear any and all unresolved issues, if you keep treating every trigger as the next layer for *you* to heal, you won't recognize your life a year from now, let alone in a decade.

Healing comes from reaching inside and holding your inner child, keeping them safe, and helping them to heal.

You don't have to let your triggers keep you stuck for the rest of your life.

If you're ready to lean in and face your past so you can heal and have a totally new life you absolutely Love, I create that safe space for you to do so (without totally going into the shitter for a decade).

You deserve to be supported. There is a new way. And no matter how lonely or lost you feel, you don't have to face it alone.

A Note From the Author

If you ever want to know whether or not you've fully processed your past, write a book about it. Notice when you're crawling out of your skin or your stomach is tied in knots. That's where you need to do your work.

A lot of people have written about their lives. But even in doing so, many of them haven't actually processed their experiences. Their book didn't bring them any closer to understanding, freedom, and peace.

That wasn't the case for me.

I used the experience of writing this book to delve even deeper into doing my work, the same work I help clients do to this day. I brought the pain from my past into present time, called back fragmented energies, shared compassion and understanding with my past self who didn't know she deserved any better, and shifted my consciousness.

It was a lot.

Even after all the work I've done, there were so many places I still had to dig in. So many chapters kicked my ass. Because I wasn't just making sure I shared my story in a Truthful, compelling way, I was facing emotions I had no idea were still stuck in my body.

A Note From the Author

By doing that work, I reached even deeper levels of connection and an even stronger willingness to be seen *and* misunderstood.

And, trust me, I know people will misunderstand me—and hopefully, if this book does its job, at a grander scale than ever before. But even that's ok. I don't need them to see me, know me, or accept me. That's my job. I can Love them exactly as and where they are—even if they don't get me.

That's why I Love this work. Because even if you don't understand it (and, in fact, a mental understanding will only get you so far), it has the power to absolutely change and transform your life forever. And I Love that for you.

Ready to do your work?

If you finished my book and thought, "I want what she's having," the good news is, you don't have to do your work alone.

I've created an online course introducing you to The Work so you can be supported when shit hits the fan and you're in too much pain to function. Hop inside Pain Isn't the End of Your Story for more. It's got everything you need to understand why you're getting your ass kicked and what to do about it.

You get to be supported and you deserve a new way.

(That's resources.ritahenry.com/pain-isnt-the-end)

Acknowledgments

When I was twenty years old, I KNEW I was going to write a book. Decades (not to mention countless really shitty drafts) and lots of life experiences later, it's finally the book my Soul wants it to be. But it wouldn't be what it is today without the help of *so* many people.

My gratitude for all of you (too many to even mention here) is beyond words. Thank you for your Love, guidance, expertise, brilliance, and delicious Americanos because they got me through the (sometimes) heartbreaking process of bringing this book to life.

To my clients and the members inside Journey to Your Center and The Healing Essentials, thank you for Loving me and for trusting me to guide you through the deepest pain to the other side. Supporting you is my greatest honor and truly is a gift.

Dr. Teri Wahlig, Dr. Bhavsar, and Dr. Sahu, thank you, thank you, thank you, for taking care of me and my girls after they were born. Your kindness, Love, and support as I lived through the hardest moments of my life were a light in the storm.

Lisa Phillips, you were there when the girls were born. You Loved me through it all and continue to do so today. You mean the world to me. I Love and appreciate you always.

Thank you, Kim Kessler, Brannan Sirratt, and Danielle Kiowski for your guidance, expertise, and editing genius. Your feedback helped shape, refine, and uplift this book. It's better for you having done your magic.

Erika Brask, thank you for this extraordinary cover and for all the ways you've cheered me on over the years. I Love your strength. Your talent is extraordinary.

Jean Graeff, thank you for bringing your brilliance to this work and my business. Your support bringing it all to life is everything.

Sheila Franzen, thank you for your wisdom, heart, and everything tech. You're an absolute genius. And whether it's with the book, business, or life, I'm stronger with you by my side. It's a joy to be your friend.

Jonathan Parker, my work with you has given me MY life. You've supported me through some of the most difficult experiences I talk about in this book. Each retreat, session, meditation, and conversation, helped me shift my consciousness and let go of the pain and struggle. Divinity is playing out having you in my life as a mentor and a dear friend.

Julia, Thomas, and Matthew, being your Mom is one of the greatest joys I'll ever experience. When you were children, I lived with many filters of pain and misunderstanding. While I'm truly sorry about that, this thing called life is messy and we learn through contrast. And I'm grateful for getting to experience it ALL with you. Thank you a bazillion times over for the gift of your Love.

Rebecca Monterusso, words can't even begin to describe how grateful I am for you and your magic. This book wouldn't exist in this form without you. It's the book my Soul wants it to be because of YOU. From ghostwriting and editing all the way through to publishing, you've elevated my story every step of the way. You've honored the work. And you've grown so much in the process. Working together feels like Divinity playing out and I can't wait to see what else we create together.

Karl Lewis, you are my Lover, husband, and friend. Thank you for Loving me through this process. The countless times you'd kiss the top of my head as you walked by or listen to me as I was in tears because this was so hard, telling me, "That's what's going to make it so good," helped me through it all. I meant everything I said in chapter 15. I LOVE Loving you.

Have Rita Visit Your Book Club

Thank you for reading *Because of Amy*. I'm absolutely honored to share my journey with you.

As a special thank you to my readers, if your book club reads this book, you're tech-savvy enough to use Zoom (or you live in the Des Moines, Iowa area), and you're interested in having me visit your book club, contact my team directly to schedule an appearance: Info@RitaHenry.com.

Appendix
Dear Diary Article, Published in the Neonatal Intensive Care Magazine

The Journal of Perinatology-Neonatology
   Neonatal Intensive Care Magazine January, February 2001 issue

The following copy was pulled from Les Plesko's editorial letter in the magazine:

While the Board is the backbone of our journal, and NICU care-givers provide the great majority of our editorial content, I thought you might be interested to see literal evidence of how your day-to-day work impacts those receiving the benefits of your care. I hope you will find our article, "Dear Diary," a piece culled from the journal of a mom who gave birth to preemie twins, as heartening as we did.

Dear Diary by Rita T. Henry

This past summer, my family and I had the privilege of seeing Dr. Vipin Bhavsar at our local Art in the Park festival in Des Moines, IA. Instantly I was taken back to August 5th, 1994, the date that Julia and Amy, our identical daughters, were born fifteen weeks prematurely. Dr. Bhavsar and Dr. Theresa Wahlig were on hand to help deliver the girls. I recall that there was supposed to be only one neonatal doctor on hand, but spirit played its hand and two doctors were present. Each girl had a wonderfully talented doctor to watch over her and to do everything in their power to help her get stabilized.

Both Julia and Amy were clinging onto life within their tiny little bodies. Amy weighed in at 1 lb 2 oz when she was born. Julia was the heavyweight at 1 lb, 8.5 oz.

So many things have transpired since that day six years ago: A funeral for Amy, a myriad of life-threatening roller coaster rides for Julia, coming to terms with how all this fit in my life, and continuous discoveries of who I am through these experiences. And now, six years later, I am so pleased that Julia is a bright, healthy girl with her whole life in front of her.

It's no wonder I lit up when I saw Dr. Bhavsar. He, along with Dr. Wahlig and Dr. Saheb Sahu, had been in my life during this very special, yet very tumultuous time. Day in and day out, their dedication to enhancing the quality of the lives of others became more and more apparent. They truly are healers. Their healing touch goes beyond the physical.

I remember their patience with me as I asked question after question about how the girls were doing and what the next steps for progress looked like. I closely monitored every medical and physical change on both of the girls. That was my way of coping.

Along with Julia and Amy, these wonderful doctors extended their expertise and patience (patients) to include me.

It has always been clear to me that Dr. Bhavsar expresses his love and his caring through his life. Indeed, his life is his message. There is a quiet strength within him. He is a gentle giant whose strength touches everyone around him.

Dr. Wahlig has a lightness of spirit that she delivers through her actions. I love the feeling and emotion she puts into her being. She is passionate about what she does and enjoys being where she is. Dr.

Wahlig embraces being a doctor, a woman and a healer. She is truly a gift.

And Dr. Sahu — oh my. I'll share more about this incredible man and how he touched my life a little later. But first I want to go back to the Art in the Park festival where we met Dr. Bhavsar. I asked him what kept him going day after day as he worked in the NICU. He pointed to 6-year-old Julia and said, "This is what keeps me going." Of course, he said he would have liked to save every baby; yet, it was such successes that helped him continue in his work.

LIFE AND DEATH

Here it is, a day later and I'm still thinking about Dr. Bhavsar and his comments. I keep playing back that part of the conversation in my mind: How he would love to save every baby, and that it was the successes that kept him going. Something about his response made me uneasy. It finally clicked. Dr. Bhavsar was putting Julia in the category of "success" because she lived, but her sister Amy (by default) was being put in the category of "unsuccessful" because she died. Hmmm.

My heart goes out to Dr. Bhavsar and to all caregivers. I understand that these wonderful people have a goal and intention on maintaining and pursuing physical life. I honor that. I respect that. I cherish that. Still, how do I share the wisdom and feelings in my heart? How do I share that the incredible quality of my life today is in direct relation to having Julia physically live and to having Amy physically die?

Yes, I know Amy will always live on in spirit and in my heart. Still, how do I explain the gift of contrast of life and death and how it has increased the quality of my life forever? Together, Julia and Amy raised the bar on the quality of my life. All for having been born. And I will forever be grateful.

No, the lessons weren't easy. No, the lessons weren't fun. Giving

Amy permission to die on that late Thursday night stands as the most difficult thing that I have ever done in my life.

Instantly, I can recall that Thursday afternoon when Dr. Sahu lovingly sat before me and bravely shared that Amy was not going to live. One of my most poignant memories is the pain I felt for Dr. Sahu. I deeply felt his heavy heart for having to share the news of Amy's impending death. I struggled to ask Dr. Sahu intellectual questions — questions of reason — questions that answered the logical, analytical side of this new turn of events. I struggled to keep the pain of my heart inside. I wanted to save Dr. Sahu from feeling the intensity of my pain.

I failed miserably. But by failing, I succeeded. For in receiving Dr. Sahu's compassion, I was validated for being real. Experiencing and expressing who I was and how I felt at that intimate moment in life was very powerful. In fact, that stands as one of the most powerful exchanges I have ever had. Dr. Sahu was gentle, patient and kind with me. He courageously connected with my spirit, never once failing to see me with his eyes, even through his own pain. His sincere offering of a hug before he left gave me courage to live with and embrace my pain. It also gave me courage to share this news with my husband, Nathan.

THANK YOU

How does one say thank you to Dr. Sahu, who came in late on that Sunday night to watch over us as our daughter died in our arms? There are no words that can fully express my feelings. It's not about words, it's about spirit, it's about connection, and it's about life.

I wonder if Dr. Sahu will ever know how much it meant to me when he came to Amy's funeral. Once again, I felt and experienced a deep connection with his spirit. A connection beyond words that encouraged me to feel beyond my self-imposed isolation. Dr. Sahu's simple hug in the parking lot of the church helped me to feel incredibly supported. I felt a little less lonely on my pain-filled path of burying several of my cherished hopes and dreams, along with my daughter.

I know at a heartfelt level that I am stronger for my experience. I love that. I know I live my life more consciously for having walked this path. I love that, too. I know that vision can only bless. I know that through this experience I have come to know myself. Huge amounts of self-knowledge came from my heart breaking wide open during this experience. Having been opened, my heart flows freely and I am open to wisdom and love that I had not seen before.

I believe it has all been a gift, all an instrumental part in my success. My success with where I am today in my roles as a mother, wife, personal coach, speaker and writer. But these roles are not who I am, these roles are what I do through my being. My being has been clarified through my experience with my daughters.

SUCCESSES

I want to share with Doctors Bhavsar, Sahu and Wahlig what I've learned: that every life they touch is a success: Even the children who don't live. We may not understand the success of a child's short life while we are in our current physical bodies. I know that even in our lack of vision, the perfection and success of a child's life is always there. Perhaps the soul of the child who moves on was there to show a mother and father how to love purely and to cherish life in a way they have never cherished it before. Or perhaps the soul of the child who moves on is there to let us know that even in our isolation we are never alone. Each soul is a gift to each of us. The gift of a child is no smaller or larger for the number of days the child lives. For spirit does not know time.

I desire for each of the doctors to feel my incredible depth of gratitude for having touched both of my girls' lives, as well as my own. When their intention is to reach out, care for, and help, that is their success. I desire for the doctors to know that their actions are directly answering the question, "What would love do now?" For their lives are the answer to that question.

Even their acceptance of their own imperfections is in response to that question. For in accepting our imperfections, that is where our perfection is experienced. It's about the lessons in life. I've come to know that it truly is the journey on the path that is the celebration of life and spirit. I cherish that.

Amy, in her physical absence, continues to share gifts with me daily that are just as significant as the ones from my other children, Matthew, Thomas and Julia. Amy is a touchstone that keeps my heart flowing ever so freely. That is success. There is no other way that I can define it. I continue to feel gratitude for this entire experience. Gratitude not only for the lessons I have learned about myself, but also for the incredibly supportive staff within the NICU who often went above and beyond their call of duty by sharing their hearts with me, as well as my daughters.

LIFE LESSONS

So, what lessons did I learn during that time in my life? Lessons about receiving. I learned how to receive from others graciously, for I would not be here today without so many reaching out to me. In my past, while I loved to give and reach out to others, I struggled with receiving from others. This experience changed my awareness of the importance of receiving fully and graciously. Today I'm still challenged with receiving at times, yet my awareness helps me in many ways.

I've learned lessons of perspective. This experience invites me to assess what is important to me in my life, within everything I do.

I've learned the lessons of pain, how, often, some incredible special gifts of life are often wrapped in pain. I learned that being with my pain allowed me to come to know and understand myself in ways I had never understood before.

There have been lessons of faith. My faith gives me hope to

believe and know everything is perfect — even in the absence of my understanding.

I have learned about self-care. Through this experience with the girls, I learned, the hard way, that unless I took care of myself in body, mind and spirit, I couldn't take care of anyone else effectively. Self-care is a lifetime commitment and is easier said than done at times. Self-care is about life balance—and even if you achieve it one day, you must still start with a clean slate the next day.

I've learned lessons about vulnerability and openness. I learned that my vulnerability and openness are my power. For in being real, I look at life with wonder and a search for Truth. Vision has no cost, it can only bless. It helps to see beyond the drama of our lives and then to seek the glorious lesson within.

These are only a few of the lessons I've learned. There are many more, and all have been life-changing. I will always be grateful. I treasure having had Doctors Bhavsar, Sahu, and Wahlig touch my life and the lives of my family. And for me, it has been an honor to have touched theirs.

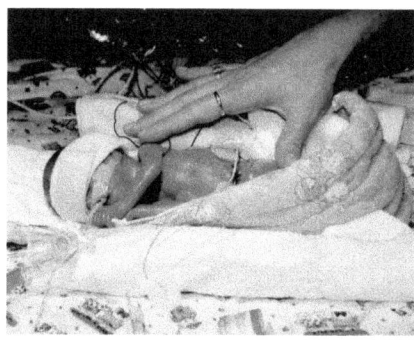

About the Author

Rita Henry is an Intuitive Guide and Healer who helps people release stored pain from their past because she's faced her own. From sexual assault to the death of her nine-day-old daughter, Rita's gotten her ass kicked by life and now helps others heal theirs.

She calls the process of seeing how you got where you are, and releasing the charged emotions keeping you held in pain, "doing your work." Doing your work shifts your consciousness and changes your brain. And on the other side, everything in your life is better (yes, even your relationship with your mother-in-law).

Rita makes it easier to do your work by naming Truth, holding a safe space for you to show up exactly as you are (messy hair, pissy pants, and all), and making energetic shifts that quiet the chaos within, so you can make peace with your troubled past and create a life you fricken' Love.

For more information, visit: www.RitaHenry.com